Great Book of Domino Games

Jennifer A. Kelley

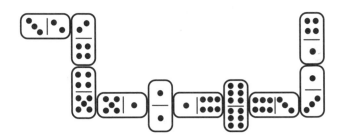

Sterling Publishing Co., Inc.
New York

Edited by Claire Bazinet

Library of Congress Cataloging-in-Publication Data

Kelley, Jennifer A.
    Great book of domino games / Jennifer A. Kelley.
        p.   cm.
    Includes index.
    ISBN 0-8069-4259-2
    1. Dominoes. I. Title.
    GV1467.K45   1999
    795.3'2—dc21   99-22533
                                                            CIP

10   9   8   7   6   5   4   3   2

Published by Sterling Publishing Company, Inc.
387 Park Avenue South, New York, N.Y. 10016
© 1999 by Jennifer A. Kelley
Distributed in Canada by Sterling Publishing
^c/o Canadian Manda Group, One Atlantic Avenue, Suite 105
Toronto, Ontario, Canada M6K 3E7
Distributed in Great Britain and Europe by Cassell PLC
Wellington House, 125 Strand, London WC2R 0BB, England
Distributed in Australia by Capricorn Link (Australia) Pty Ltd.
P.O. Box 6651, Baulkham Hills, Business Centre, NSW 2153, Australia
Manufactured in the United States of America

Sterling ISBN 0-8069-4259-2

*My inspiration came first from my
always-supportive parents:
my schoolteacher mother, Mary Lou Howell,
and my journalist father, Larry Howell.
Thanks to both of you and to my entire family,
who were all a huge help in this venture.*

Acknowledgments

I would like to thank the following domino book authors (some are also domino game creators): R.C. Bell (*Discovering Dice and Dominoes*); Gary M. Grady and Suzanne Goldberg (Dominoes "Rules of the Games" series); Lloyd McLeod (*Dominoes Texas Style*); Dennis Roberson (*Winning 42: Strategy and Lore of the National Game of Texas*); Mary D. Lankford (*Dominoes Around the World*) and Charles B. Wallace (*Win at Dominoes*). I owe a special thank-you to Victor T. Lewis, who inspired *me* to write my own book on domino games.

After contacting his publisher, I searched extensively, to no avail, for Fredrick Berndt, author of *The Domino Book* (Thomas Nelson, 1974). I have included here a few of his games. Mr. Berndt, if you're out there, please contact me. I'd love to talk dominoes with you.

I would also like to thank the following domino game creators for permission to include their tile games: David Crump; David Galt; Edna Graham; Charles T. Gravley; Betty Howsley at Howsley's Fox Creek Store; Roy and Katie Parsons; Michael Poor at Intellitoy; and Ferman Rice. My thanks also go to the following domino manufacturers and distributors for all their wonderful help: Bonnie Tanner at Cardinal Industries; Bill Chiu and David Kessler at Plastech Industries; Hudson Dobson at Gamesource Limited; Lori Long at Creative Teaching Associates; and, Charles T. Chiang of Domino32. A special thanks is in order to Scott Pitzer of Puremco Dominoes. I am so grateful to Scott for the generosity of his time and knowledge. I gained such a respect for him as a businessman and as a person over the months of working with him.

Thanks also to: Bill Schuler and Marian Morrissey of the International Domino Association; Clive Wilson of the Jamaican Library; Sallie Desmond; Gayle Todd of the Coon Hunters Domino Club; Joseph Madachy of *The Journal of Recreational Mathematics*; Cindy Hillman and Kyle McAlister, children of the late George McAlister, co-author of *Dominoes Texas Style*; Barbara Brumley, daughter of Lloyd McLeod, co-author of *Dominoes Texas Style*; Fred Armanino, relative of, and Mrs. Dominic C. Armanino, former wife to, the late Dominic C. Armanino, author of several domino game instruction books; Shire Publications Ltd., UK, publisher of R.C. Bell's book *Discovering Dice and Dominoes*; Ken Tidwell of Game Cabinet; David Koehler; Ed Pellon, and the Editors and Jess Brallier at the former Planet Dexter.

Thanks also to Joe Celko. I am looking forward to your domino game book.

The domino graphics for this book were done by Darryl Stein of Stein Graphics. Thank you, Darryl.

Contents

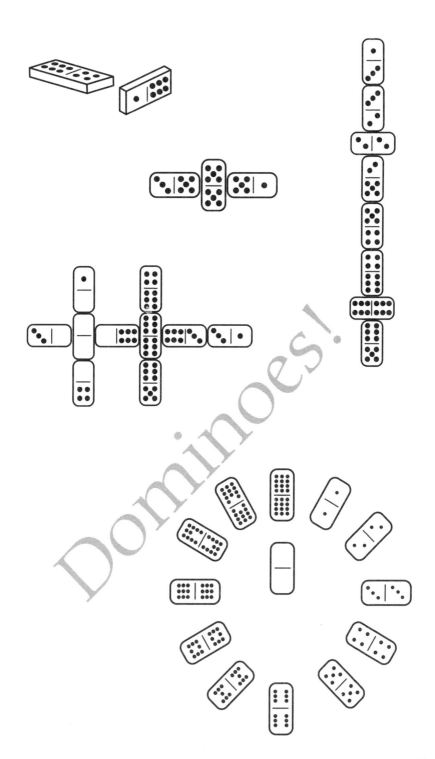

Foreword

Many adults enjoy playing with dominoes. Some like the competition; for others, it's simply a relaxing way to pass the time with friends. Children love to play dominoes, too. It's a great way for them to learn important math skills, because it makes learning interesting and fun. It also gives them an opportunity to develop good sportsmanship.

Domino games can provide hours of entertainment for the entire family. Most games are easy to learn and include elements of both skill and chance. Playing dominoes is a way to exercise your mind and a pleasurable, fun activity to enjoy with friends.

Whether you enjoy playing dominoes when you're by yourself or at a party with as many as eight or more players; whether you're very young, a beginner, or an experienced dominoes player, you'll find a wide assortment of games here to choose from.

All you need for most games is a set of dominoes and a flat playing surface, like a table or a board. Most domino sets are fairly inexpensive and will last a lifetime. So, what are you waiting for? Let's play!

A SMALL WORLD

I have three American friends who come from different parts of the world: Moscow, Iraq (he's Kurdish), and Mexico City. They moved to the United States after living at least twenty years in other countries. Yet, in response to my questions about domino play in their native countries, they amazingly all essentially described to me the same basic game, "Block."

I say "amazingly" because, in researching domino game names and rules for this book, I found very many different variations to many different variations of variations! I searched out games from around the globe and organized them into categories, and sub-categories! After going through hundreds of different domino games, and even hundreds more ways of playing those different domino games, I realized I was discovering the same domino games over and over again. Yes, it is a small world!

Getting back to my friends, the one from Moscow said the domino game he remembers is called "Kozel" in Russian, which translates to "Goat." My Kurdish friend told me about the tea shops in Iraq where men pass the time playing dominoes with friends, drinking tea, and just generally "hanging out." My friend from Mexico said the game there is nearly always played with partners. Perhaps one reason is that, in Mexico, communication between partners—the use of a special code-language to alert your partner that you hold a good hand, a bad hand, you don't hold the tile he or she needs, and so on—is considered a skill to be mastered. In the United States, on the other hand, any kind of such communication between partners in any form is considered cheating and, in tournament play, is absolutely *not* tolerated! Even small worlds do have their differences.

Introduction to Dominoes

The Pieces

Domino pieces are sometimes called tiles, rocks, blocks, stones, bones, men, or seeds.

Small, flat, rectangular-shaped game pieces made of plastic, wood, bone, ivory, stone, or other material, they are usually twice as long as they are wide. The tiles in most sets are made to be exactly half as thick as they are wide so that they can stand on edge without falling over. A domino may be of any size, but an ordinary domino is about one inch wide and two inches long.

Like a playing card, a domino has a *face* and a *back*. The back of each tile is either blank or the back of every tile in the set is decorated with an identical design. The face of each tile is divided by a line across the center separating the piece into two halves. Numbers are represented in each half by spots, commonly called *pips*, or the absence of spots, which represents zero. A half that doesn't have pips is called a zero, blank, pale, or white.

When dominoes are made, the pips are uniformly molded or drilled and then painted. The pips are usually black if the tile is white; white, if the tile is black. However, domino sets can be found in almost any color combination.

A DOMINO FACE

This domino face has 1 pip on one half and 6 pips on the other half and is called the 1-6 domino. Dominoes with the same number of pips on each half of the face are known as *doubles* or *doublets*. A *single* domino, also referred to as a *combination* domino, has a different number of pips on each half of the face. All the tiles in a set of dominoes that have the same number of pips (or the absence of any) on one end make up a *suit*. For example, the 0-0, 0-1, 0-2, 0-3, 0-4, 0-5, and 0-6 pieces make up the suit of zero. Each double belongs to only one suit; singles belong to two suits. For example, the 1-6 belongs to the 1 suit and the 6 suit. Dominoes are also thought of as having *weights*. A domino is heavier than another domino if it has more pips. A domino is lighter if it has fewer pips.

In most domino games, the number of pips on a domino are added or subtracted for scoring purposes. In some domino games, however, the number of pips on a domino are used strictly for matching purposes. In these matching games, dominoes with pictures, colors, or shapes on each half of the domino face could be used just as easily as dominoes with pips. Many domino sets made for children have colorful pictures on the face of each domino instead of pips.

The Domino Set

A set of domino pieces is sometimes called a *deck*. The three most common domino sets are the double-6, double-9, and double-12 sets. The set is named after the domino in the set with the highest number of pips. Most domino games are designed to be played with the double-6 set.

Every set of dominoes includes all possible combinations of two numbers, from zero (blank) up to the highest number of pips in the set (for example, 12 in a double-12 set), as well as a double for each suit. Each combination of pips occurs only once in a set.

A standard double-6 domino set consists of 28 tiles: 7 doubles and 21 singles.

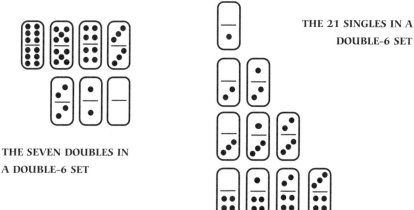

THE 21 SINGLES IN A
DOUBLE-6 SET

THE SEVEN DOUBLES IN
A DOUBLE-6 SET

In a double-6 set, each number appears eight times: once each on six tiles and twice on the double tile. A double-9 set consists of 55 tiles, with each number appearing 11 times. A double-12 set consists of 91 tiles, with each number appearing 14 times. A double-15 set of tiles is the latest to hit the market—and with phenomenal success.

The Stock and Hands

The set of dominoes from which a player draws his hand before the game and the tiles remaining, which are drawn from throughout the game when necessary, is called the stock, the boneyard, the kitty, or the reserve.

Most domino games are played with *hands*. The unplayed tiles each player holds in his possession make up his hand. Before the game, each player picks tiles from the stock to make up his hand. In some domino games, it may be the rule to add more tiles to your hand throughout the game by picking them from the stock. Every time a player makes a play, a tile is subtracted from his hand and, when the game is over, the tiles left in the player's possession, if any, are also considered his hand. (The word "hand" also often refers to the series of plays from when the first domino is set to when a player "dominoes." A game of dominoes will comprise several such hands.)

MODIFYING

Many games can easily be modified for play with other sets, or vice versa. To modify a set, tiles from the double-6 set can be removed to create a double-5 set or a double-3 set, for example, if that is what you need to play. Or tiles from the double-12 set can be removed to create a double-10 set. Just make sure that your "created" set contains all the possible combinations of two numbers, from zero (blank) up to the highest number of pips in the set, as well as a double for each suit. Each combination of pips occurs only once in a set.

The obvious reason for modifying the rules to be played with a different set is that you don't have the set called for. There are, however, other reasons: 1) it can change the level of difficulty of the game; 2) it can accommodate more players or fewer players; and, 3) it can shorten or lengthen a game. So, you have lots of options to choose from.

History of Domino Games

The actual origin of the game of dominoes—who invented the game and where and when it was first played—is unknown. There is evidence that a version of the basic matching game, where plays are match tiles end to end, was played in the Far East in ancient times, but the basic matching game that we know today first appeared in Italy in the eighteenth century. From Italy, the game seems to have spread to France and then was brought to England by prisoners of war about 1790. In 1801, Joseph Strutt, in his book *Sports and Pastimes of the People of England*, expressed his view of one of the most popular games of that period. The game simply went by the name "Dominoes," and he described it as "a very childish sport, imported from France a few years back."

Some attempts have been made to trace the entry of dominoes into Europe from the Far East, perhaps through the Middle East, but so far no clear-cut connection has been established. As far as can be determined by historical evidence, dominoes seem to have existed in the Far East long before they appeared in the West. This does not necessarily mean, however, that there is a direct connection. The relatively elementary concept of the basic matching game played with dominoes may well have evolved in Europe quite independently, especially in view of its possible connection with dice.

Dominoes—the pieces and the rules of play—are known throughout the Orient. Only the Chinese, however, have left us with much of a history, and a good part of that may be legendary.

According to some accounts, domino pieces can be traced to Hung Ming, a soldier-hero who lived from A.D. 181 to 234. Others attribute it to the ingenuity of Keung T'ai Kung in the 12th century B.C. The *Chu sz yam*, "Investigations on the Traditions of All Things," states that domino pieces were invented in A.D. 1120 by a statesman who presented them to the Emperor Hui Tsung, and that they were circulated abroad by imperial order during the reign of Hui Tsung's son, Kao Tsung (A.D. 1127–1163). Other interpreters of this document, however, maintain that it refers not to the invention of domino pieces and a particular game played with those pieces but to the standardization of domino pieces and game rules; domipieces and games played with dominoes having been in existence long before that. All in all, there is no historical evidence which points conclusively to the invention of the first domino games. Most likely, as is the came with most games, the rules to the games evolved gradually rather than being a singular invention.

Mah-jongg, a game for four people which uses 144 pieces, originated in China and by 1400, it has spread all over China. Some people consider mah-jongg to be the "great-grandfather" of dominoes. R.C. Bell, an English game researcher, believes that dominoes were clearly a Chinese invention. Others see Arabia as the country of origin. In Egypt, it's still one of the most popular café games.

Dominoes became popular in coffee houses during the nineteenth century, and in 1820 a book by C. van Greeven was published in Dutch at The Hague. It was entitled *Het bedrog, hetwelk men met het zogenaamde domino-spel pleegt, ontmaskerd*—which translates to "The deceits that people commit at the so-called game of dominoes unmasked."

Dominoes are not mentioned in *Hoyle's Games Improved* (1814). Even in the 1853 edition, *Hoyle's Games Improved and Enlarged*, the game merits only a page and a half, with the entry starting: "Domino [note the singular form] is played by 2 to 4 persons with 28 pieces of oblong ivory, plain at the back, but in the face divided by a black line in the middle and indented with spots from one to a double-6." A lengthy description of the individual pieces then follows. In all the early pieces

WORD ORIGIN OF "DOMINO"

The word domino was probably derived from the Latin word *dominus*, which means "the master of the house." The vocative *domine* became the Scottish and English dominic (schoolmaster), and the dative or ablative *domino* became the French, then the English, *domino*, which referred at first to a sort of monastic hood; then to a hooded masquerade costume with a small mask; then to the mask itself; and finally to one of the pieces in the game. It thus became dominoes, presumably from the fancied resemblance between a mask and one or more of the pieces, probably the 1-1. The word domino was accepted by the Académie Française in 1798 as the name of the game and the name of the pieces.

seen by the author, however, the "ivory" was bone. The account also contains the remark "Sometimes a double set is played with, of which double-12 is the highest." The game described is "The Block Game." Hoyle's short entry ends with this admonition: "This game requires strict attention, and nothing but practice will make perfect."

History of Domino Pieces

The ancients used sticks, stones, and bones as a way of adding. Perhaps, later, they may have used flat rocks, bones, or pieces of wood with dots to represent numbers counted. As man began to communicate verbally, he gave names to the numbers and developed a counting system as high as the number of fingers and toes he had. Thus, the objects used for tallying may have had dots up to 20.

As civilizations progressed, merchants used stacks of rocks for computing. Later, the Babylonians used clay tiles for counting. A stylus was used to press cuneiform numerals on the clay tiles. These tiles could have been used to keep a record of business transactions in banking or taxes. It takes only a minor stretch of the imagination to see the tiles being transformed into pieces with which to play games.

The Greeks and the Hindus used the 10-numeral (decimal) system for counting. About A.D. 500, a Hindu devised a positional notation for the numerals. The Hindus modernized the first nine symbols from 1 to 9. The zero came in use about A.D. 825, when an Arab mathematician of Baghdad recommended that Hindu numerals be used by merchants and mathematicians of both East and West. With the development of the numerals from 1 to 9, objects similar to dominoes and dice were used in our counting system. After the zero was added, the 21-domino set got the blanks for a suit; thus our standard set of 28 dominoes was formed and used for games and counting in business.

By the thirteenth century, our humble objects of the numerals came to Italy from the trade conducted by long Arab caravans to India and China. Dominoes may have been introduced into the business of Europe at that time. In the fifteenth century, objects similar to dominoes were used to teach arithmetic at a private school in Mantua, Italy. The use of dominoes for games and objects of counting in trading and banking continued to develop in the cities of Venice, Florence, and Genoa.

The earliest dominoes were made of rectangles of bone with plain backs and pips drilled into the fronts. Many were made by French prisoners of war from mutton and beef bones and were sold to augment the prisoners' meager allowances. Others were the work of seamen, whiling away their leisure hours on long voyages. Some of these sets were novelty items, including then well-known "birdcage sets."

Suitable thick pieces of bone were scarce, necessitating the use of thinner pieces fastened onto an ebony backing with glue and a central brass sprig. Later, other hardwoods were stained to simulate ebony, and the central sprig was reinforced with two smaller sprigs.

In 1855, Charles Lepage of Paris invented *bois durci*, a substitute for wood, bone, metal, and other hard substances, consisting of rosewood or ebony sawdust and albumen from eggs and blood. The sawdust was soaked in pure albumen and water; the mixture was then dried and placed in a steel mold and subjected to heat and pressure in a hydraulic press. *Bois durci* domino sets, or even single pieces, are now rare and are desirable collectors' items.

Bois durci, the first plastic, was followed a year later by celluloid, originally known as Parkesine and now called Xylonite. This material was first made by Parkes of Birmingham in 1856 and used for dominoes, but unfortunately it was highly flammable. In the late nineteenth century, cheap domino sets were made of tinplate for use in public houses, and were often provided at nominal cost or even free by tobacco companies.

Bakelite appeared about 1910, named after Dr. Leo Baekeland, the inventor. Made from phenols and formaldehyde, this synthetic resin could be poured, cast and molded. Bakelite quickly came into popular use for carved jewelry. Dominoes were also made using the new material, as was important automobile electrical insulation. The Bakelite patent expired in 1927 and was acquired by Catalin Corporation. Bakelite-Catalin was used to make molded radio cases as well as carved jewelry and, of course, dominoes. Bakelite and Catalin became obsolete after World War II with the advent of injection and compression-molded plastics.

Colored sheets of Perspex, though expensive, can be used to make attractive dominoes that are pleasant to the touch. Black and white sheets of Perspex are cemented together then cut into rectangles and the pips are hand-drilled and painted.

Today, all mass-produced dominoes are made either of wood, urea compression molded plastic, or poured marblelike polyester resin. Wooden dominoes with designs impressed on their backs, largely made in South America, are inexpensive for children's toys. The most popular dominoes for adult games are made of urea plastic, from China, or marblelike resin by Puremco, a Texas company. Domino sets today are available in several colors, including ivory, and even specially personalized.

As for domino play, there's little difference around the world, and new games will undoubtedly be created in the years ahead, so whenever you travel and find a friendly game in progress, be an onlooker for a while then join in and try your skill. Whatever its derivation, dominoes is a fantastic game. Our thanks for many entertaining hours should go to the unknowns who first invented the tiles and the game.

Domino Terms

Ace   The end of a tile with one pip.

Arm   A row of dominoes set in a straight line in the layout of a matching or scoring game.

Bid   The number of points a player in a bidding game anticipates making for that hand. The player winning the bid (highest bidder) earns the right to name the trumps and also make the first play of the hand.

Block   1) In a matching or scoring game, the process of playing a domino which cannot be followed in suit by your opponent. 2) Domino pieces are sometimes called *blocks*. 3) Another name for the Block Game.

Blocked Game   In a matching or scoring game, if 1) no player is able to make a play; 2) draw from the boneyard; and, 3) all players are still holding tiles in their hand, the game is said to be "blocked." At which time the game is over and is said to have "ended in block."

Blocking Games   Games in which scoring is done only at the end of each hand and not after individual plays are made. Play is aimed at blocking your opponent and being the first player to play all the tiles in your hand.

Count Dominoes   1) In bidding games, the tiles that have pips that total 5 or a multiple of 5. If playing with one set of double-6 tiles, for example, the count dominoes would include the 5-5 and 6-4 (each worth 10 points) and the 5-0, 3-2, and 4-1 (each worth 5 points). 2) In scoring games, tiles played so that the sum of the pips on the exposed ends of the layout total 5 or a multiple of 5.

Cutthroat   1) Any domino game in which each player plays independently, for himself, without a partner. 2) A 3-handed game or any game with 4 or more players in which each player plays for himself, without a partner. 3) The name of a 4-handed, Texas-style game of dominoes, in which each player plays for himself, without a partner.

Deuce   The end of a tile with two pips.

Domino   1) One of the pieces, or tiles, in a set of dominoes. 2) In matching and scoring games, to be the first player to play the last tile in his hand, and therefore, win that hand. **Dominoed**   When a person is the first to play the last tile in his hand, he is said to have "dominoed."

Dominoer The person playing the last remaining domino in his hand.

Go Out When a player is the first to play the last tile in his hand in a matching or scoring game.

Head Up A game of dominoes played by only two players.

Leader 1) The player who plays first, puts down the first tile. 2) In a matching or scoring game, a double tile played when the player has no matching dominoes in his hand.

Round Games 1) "Party games" for a large group of people. 2) Games in which each player plays for himself.

Scoring Games Games in which scores are made during play and at the end of the hand.

Set 1) In a bidding game, if a player cannot make his bid, he is said to be "set." 2) In matching and scoring games, the first tile played.

Spinner 1) A double in the layout which may played on both sides and both ends. Matching and scoring games each have a rule about spinners: a) There are no spinners; b) Only the first double played is a spinner; or c) All doubles are spinners. 2) In games where only the first double played is a spinner, "spinner" refers to the first double played.

Suit(s) Dominoes having the same number of pips on one end. For example: the 0-6, 1-6, 2-6, etc., are all from the 6 suit.

Trey The end of a tile with three pips.

Trick A term used in bidding games. In the game of Forty-Two, for example, each of the four players plays 1 tile per trick. The trick is won by the player who played the winning tile of the 4 tiles played. There are 7 tricks in the game of Forty-Two.

Trumps 1) In bidding games, the winning bidder earns the opportunity to name trumps for that hand. The word "trump" comes from the word "triumph." A domino from the trump suit automatically "triumphs" over other dominoes played. 2) Doubles are sometimes referred to as "trumps."

Widow or Widows The tile, or tiles, left after each player has drawn hands from the deck at the beginning of a hand. Also called "the boneyard." However, the term "the boneyard" is typically used in matching and scoring games and usually refers to tiles that are purposely not drawn at the beginning of the game, so that players can draw from the boneyard during the game when they do not hold a playable tile in their hand. The term "widow(s)" is typically used in bidding games and usually refers to the tile or tiles left after all players have drawn their hands from the deck at the beginning of the hand and there are "widow(s)" because the number of tiles cannot be divided equally among the number of players.

Domino Rules: The Basics

You may already play some domino games. If so, you may find that the rules here are not exactly the same as those you have learned. Many domino games go by different names yet have extremely similar, sometimes even identical, rules. Also, many games go by the same name in various parts of the world, but the rules vary from place to place.

I have tried to make this book as complete as possible, including every variation to every game for which I was able to find rules. Whether you follow the rules precisely, or whichever variation of any game you choose to use, is irrelevant as long as all the players clearly understand what the rules of play are and agree to them before a game begins. It is also, of course, important to be sure the rules you choose to play by are functional. Even so, a situation may arise in play that is not covered by any rule in this book. In such a case, it may be necessary for the players to agree on a workable rule to cover the problem.

The basic rules in this chapter apply to most of the games in this book, but not all of them. For example, there are a few games included where hands are not drawn and, of course, the basic rules that pertain to more than one player would not apply to solitaire games.

In many domino games, as players make their plays, a line of tiles is formed on the table usually, but not always, by matching the pips on the open end of the domino. This formation of tiles is called the line of play. There are basic instructions listed here under "Line of Play" specifically for those games.

Shuffling the Tiles

Before every game, a player shuffles the tiles facedown on a flat playing surface, thoroughly mixing them by moving them with his hands. The player's hands may not remain on the same tiles while shuffling, and the player doing the shuffling should be the last to draw his hand for the game.

Players may choose to take turns shuffling before each game or the same player may shuffle the dominoes before each game. Here are two of several options: 1) The player to the right of the player making the first play does the shuffling for a game; or 2) The winner of the previous game shuffles for the next game.

Seating Arrangement

A player's position at the table in a game with three or more players is called a *seat*.

One way to determine seating arrangements is by lot. After the tiles are shuffled, each player draws a domino from the stock. The player who draws the tile with the greatest number of pips (the heaviest tile) has the first choice of seating. The player holding the next highest seats himself to the left, and so on. If there is a tie, it is broken by drawing new dominoes from the stock. The tiles are returned to the stock and reshuffled before the players draw their hands. When a partnership game is played, the partners sit opposite each other.

Setting Order of Play

There are several different ways to determine which player will make the first play: You can draw lots, begin the game by setting the heaviest domino, or have the winner of the previous game make the first play of the next game. After it is determined who will make the first play of the game, the order of play will be decided by the seating arrangement. Play will continue to the left, clockwise, after the first play is made. Or, you may choose to play in a counterclockwise rotation, as is done in some Latin American countries, as long as all players agree to it before the game.

Drawing lots to determine first play: After the tiles are shuffled, each player draws a domino from the stock. The player who draws the heaviest tile will make the first play. If there is a tie, it is broken by drawing new dominoes from the stock.

Begin by setting heaviest domino: In some domino games, the rules state that the first play must be made by the player with the highest double in his hand. Rules for other games state that the first play must be made by the player with the heaviest domino, double or single, as the case may be.

If *highest double*, after the tiles are shuffled, each player draws his hand from the stock. The player who draws the highest double of the set (i.e., double-9 if playing with a double-9 set), plays it as the lead. If the highest double was not drawn, the second-highest double is played. If the second-highest double was not drawn, the third-highest double is played, and so on, until a double is played. If none of the players holds a double in his hand, all hands are discarded, reshuffled, and new hands are drawn. After the first player sets his double, the second play is made by the player to his left and play continues clockwise.

If *heaviest tile*, follow the instructions above for highest double with this exception: Instead of drawing new hands if no player holds a double tile, the player holding the heaviest single begins play.

Winner of last game goes first: The winner of the last game played may open the next game. Or, if a game ends in a tie, the player who placed the last tile plays the first tile in the next game.

Drawing the Hand

Each player draws the number of tiles specified in the rules for the domino game being played and then positions them in front of himself in such a way that the other players cannot see the pips on his tiles.

After all hands have been drawn, there may be a surplus of tiles left in the stock. These tiles should remain facedown and, depending on the rules of the game being played, may be bought later in that game (see "Passing and Buying" below).

Opening the Game

Determine who will make the first play as explained above and according to the rules of the particular domino game being played. The player making the first play may be referred to as the setter, the downer, or the leader. He should place his tile faceup in the middle of the table.

The words set, down, and lead are all used as verbs to refer to the act of making the first play of the game. "The set," "the down," and "the lead" are used as nouns to refer to the first domino played in a game and also the first play of the game.

Here is a rule variation that players may agree to employ: Any time a player plays a double, whether for the opening of the game or during the play of the game, he may immediately play a *second* tile onto his double before the next player makes his play.

Passing and Buying

Any player who does not hold in his hand a tile with the correct number of pips, and therefore cannot make the next play, must either pass or buy from the stock, according to the rules of the game. Some games permit players to skip a play if they so choose, even if they hold a playable tile.

Passing is also called knocking or renouncing. A player unable to make a play must announce to the other players "I pass"; then the next player takes his turn. If no one is able to make a play, the game ends.

In some games, buying tiles from the stock is allowed. In this case, a player draws the number of tiles he is permitted to take according to the rules of that game, adding them to the tiles he is holding in his hand. Once the player has drawn a tile he is able to play, he plays that domino.

There are many domino games that have the rule that all tiles in the stock may be bought, and there are others that have the rule that some tiles must be left in the stock and cannot be bought. In the case of the latter, the number of pips on the tiles left in the stock at the end of the game are added to the winner's score.

Line of Play

There are many domino games that depend upon matching suits. In these games, the first player sets his domino, then the player to his left adds his tile to one of the free ends, and so on, going clockwise around the table with each player adding a tile. Players add tiles that have the matching number of pips with an open end of an already played tile.

As each player matches and plays a tile, a line is formed. This configuration of dominoes is called the layout, string, or line of play. In order to prevent tiles from falling off the table when the line of play extends too far, dominoes may be played in any direction. Regardless of the pattern of the line of play, the open end of the last domino played remains the same.

Dominoes are joined to the line of play in two ways: 1) with the line of play, lengthwise (dominoes played end to end) or 2) across the line of play, crosswise (dominoes played across the matching number). In most domino games, doubles and *only* doubles are played crosswise; singles are played lengthwise. The next tile added after each double played, if the double is not a spinner, must be lengthwise.

Spinners: A spinner is a double that can be played on all four sides. Depending on the rules of the game being played,

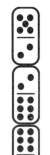

the double played as the lead is the only spinner of the game; *or* every double played throughout the game is a spinner. If the double played is not a spinner, it may be played on only two sides.

Scoring: In some domino games, part of the score is obtained from the total number of pips at the ends of the line of play as the game progresses. If only one domino has been played, both ends of that domino are ends of the line of play. Thus, if a 5-5 tile is played, the count would be 10.

If two dominoes have been played, the count depends on whether both tiles are with the line of play or one tile is with and the other tile is across the line of play. For example, if the 3-5 and 5-1 tiles are played, the count is 4 (3+1). The matching halves of each of the two dominoes would be joined, end to end, with the open ends being 3 and 1). If the 3-5 and 5-5 tiles are played, the count is 13 (3+5+5). The double tile, 5-5, would be played across the line of play, and both halves of the double would be considered ends of the line of play.

Given the last example, if a tile is now played on the 5-5, assuming it is not a spinner, the 5-5 is no longer an end for the purpose of counting. See the example below. The line of play is 3-5, 5-5, 5-1, and the count is 4 (3+1). If the 5-5 is not a spinner in this case, the 5-5 is not an end.

In some domino games, a score is made only when the count of the ends of the line of play is a multiple of 5 or a multiple of 3, for example.

Another scoring method used in many domino games is to take the losing players' total number of pips by counting the pips on the tiles left in their hands at the end of a hand or the game and then adding that number to the winner's score.

Here is a rule variation that players may agree to employ: When counting the pips on the tiles left in the losers' hands at the end of a hand or the game, count only one end of a double (e.g., 4-4 counts as only 4 points).

End of the Game

Some domino games end once a certain number of hands have been played or a player or team makes the necessary points to win. For many other domino games, the object of the game is to be the first player (or team) to dispose of all the dominoes in hand. These domino games end when a player has played all the dominoes in his or her hand and summarily announces, "Domino."

Sometimes none of the players are able to make another play. This is called a *blocked game*, and, in case the game is blocked and no one is able to make another play, the game would end.

If Accidents Occur

During a game, there will be times when errors or misplays will occur. Here are general rules for handling some common accidents.

Dominoes exposed in error: If your domino is accidentally exposed to another player, it must then be exposed to all of the players.

Too many tiles drawn: If a player draws more tiles for his hand than he is entitled to, it is called an *overdraw*. Once an overdraw has been discovered, the player to the right of the overdrawn hand takes the extra dominoes from the overdrawn hand, without looking at them, and returns them to the stock. The deck should then be reshuffled before anyone else draws his hand. (Here is a rule variation that players may agree to employ: Expose the overdrawn tiles to all players before returning them to the stock and then reshuffle the deck.)

Not enough tiles drawn: If a player draws fewer tiles than he or she is entitled to for a hand, it is called an *underdraw*. Once an underdraw has been discovered, the player draws the necessary tiles from the stock to complete the hand.

Domino played in error: When a player plays the wrong domino, it is called a *misplay*. If a player misplays (for example, joins a 2 to a 3) and it is discovered before the next play is made, the misplayer must restore the incorrect tile to his hand and play a correct one. If a player misplays and no one notices until after the next play has been made, the wrong tile is considered played and cannot be replaced with the correct tile. If a score is realized on the undiscovered misplay, the player is allowed to keep it.

If a play is not a misplay, once a tile is played and a player takes his hand off the tile, it may not be taken up again by the player.

Play out of turn: When a player plays out of turn, it is also called a misplay. If a player plays out of turn and it is discovered before the next player makes his play, he must recall his tile. If a player plays out of turn and it is not discovered before the next play, the misplay must stand. If a score is realized on the misplay, the player is allowed to keep it.

Types of Domino Games

Nearly all of the most popular domino games fit into one of four categories: bidding games, blocking games, scoring games, and round games.

Bidding games: Bidding games are cardlike games, played by two to four players. In these games, players bid their hands, the highest bidder names the suit, and the score is determined by the bid.

Blocking games: Blocking games are played by matching dominoes in a line. Scoring is done only at the end of each hand. The player or team who plays all the dominoes in his hand first, or "dominoes," scores the total count of the tiles still held by his opponent(s). In the event of a blocked game, the player or team who has the lowest count scores the total count of the tiles still held by his opponent(s).

Scoring games: A scoring game, like a blocking game, is also played by matching dominoes. One difference is that scoring is done throughout the game after each scoring play is made, as well as at the end of each hand. The game is played until a player or team makes the necessary points to win. A game consists of a series of hands. A hand consists of a series of plays with the dominoes drawn from the deck.

Games for Two or More Players

BLOCKING GAMES

All of the games in this section have certain things in common: First, points are scored at the end of each hand, therefore there is no regard to the end count. Play is aimed, instead, at blocking your opponent from making a play. The game of Block and the game of Draw are two of the most simple and basic of all domino games. Many games are variations of one of these games. In both of these games, plays are made by matching suits with one of the tiles in your hand to one of the open ends in the line of play. The object of the game is to be the first player to domino.

The game of Block and the game of Draw are identical with one exception: In the game of Draw you draw extra dominoes from the boneyard if you are unable to make a play. In the game of Block you do *not* draw extra dominoes from the boneyard if you are unable to make a play. This seems to be the most widely used description of the difference between the game of Block and the game of Draw. However, in some places, the rules for a game called "Block" are that players draw from the boneyard when unable to make a play.

The game of Block is also known as Block Dominoes, the Block Game, and Allies (Block with Partners). The game of Draw also goes by the names Draw Dominoes, Draw Game, the Draw or Block Game, Block Dominoes with Buying, and even Domino Big Six, and Double-Six Dominoes.

The game of Doubles is sometimes called Maltese Cross. However, in all but one place, the rules I found to Maltese Cross did not contain the rule that makes Doubles a unique game: sometimes tiles cannot be played until the double of that suit has already been played. For that reason, I have listed these two games separately in this section.

Because all the games here are basically variations of Block, I have provided, under the heading "What's unique," details differentiating these Block games' variations from each other. Unless otherwise indicated, the following rules apply to each of the games below:
- One set of double-6 dominoes (28 pieces) is used.
- The dominoes are shuffled, facedown, at the beginning of each hand.
- The object of the game is to be the first player to domino.

Block

(aka Block Dominoes, the Block Game, and Allies)

Number of players: Best for 2 to 4 players.

Number of dominoes drawn: For 2 to 4 players, each player draws 7 tiles. If 5 or more are playing, prior to the start of the game players should determine and agree upon the number of tiles each player should draw from the deck. (If 2 players, each draws 7 or 8 tiles; 3 or 4 players, draw 5 or 6 tiles.)

If there are any remaining tiles after the draw, they are discarded, not used during that hand because there will be no drawing from the boneyard.

Set domino: Any domino may be used. Variations: 1) highest double, and in the event no double is drawn, re-shuffle and re-draw; 2) 6-6, and in the event the 6-6 is not drawn, re-shuffle and re-draw; or, 3) highest double, and in the event no double is drawn, play the highest single. After a tile has been set, play continues to the left.

How to play: Each player tries to match the pips on one end of a tile from his hand with the pips on an open end of any tile in the layout. If a player is unable to match a tile from his hand with a tile in the layout, the player passes his turn to the player on his left. Each player may play only one tile per turn.

The first player to get rid of all dominoes announces "Domino!" and wins the game. If none of the players can make a play, the game ends in a block. If a game ends in a block, all the players turn the tiles in their hands faceup, count the pips on each tile, and add them together. The player with the lowest total wins the game and earns the points (1 point per pip) of all the tiles left remaining in his opponents' hands. The player who first reaches 100 points or more is the overall winner.

Other rules: The game can be played with no spinners (which seems the most often used rule) or by using the first double as the only spinner of the game.

In most places, Block is played to 100 points. However, there are many different variations, including to 50, 150, 200, or 101 points.

Draw

(aka Draw Dominoes, the Draw Game, the Draw or Block Game, Block Dominoes with Buying, Domino Big Six, and Double-Six Dominoes)

Draw is the same as Block, with these exceptions:

After each player draws his hand from the deck, the remaining tiles are pushed to one side to make up the boneyard.

If a player cannot match a tile with one in the layout, he must draw from the boneyard until he picks a tile that can be played. He must keep the tiles he drew but couldn't use on that play. If there are no tiles left in the boneyard, the player passes his turn to the player on his left.

Mexican Train

(© 1994 by Roy and Katie Parsons)

Number of players/domino set: 2 to 4 players using the double-9 set (55 tiles); 5 to 8 players using the double-12 set (91 tiles). Adaptations can be easily made should your players/sets not exactly fit this guideline. Double-15 sets (136 tiles) can be used for even larger groups.

Additional equipment: A score sheet and one small marker per player (i.e., penny, dried bean, poker chip).

Object of the game: To rid your hand of as many dominoes as possible and to be the first to do this. The other players then must total the points or pips remaining in their hands and keep a running total for their score. The lowest score wins.

To begin, pull out the 12-12 if playing with a double-12 set (or the 9-9 if playing with a double-9 set) from the deck. This domino is called the "engine" and will be the centerpiece/starter for this game. Place the engine in the center of the table. Shuffle the remaining dominoes face down.

Number of tiles drawn: 2 players draw 12 tiles each; 3 players draw 11; 4 players draw 10; 5 players draw 12; 6 players draw 11;

7 players draw 10; and 8 players draw 9. Additional players can play by adjusting this numerical arrangement to fit.

Players draw their number of tiles with the remaining tiles set aside in "bonepiles," to be drawn as needed later in the game.

The players then organize the tiles in their hands in a playable progression beginning with the same number as the engine/centerpiece. The tile ends must match and form a line to be ready to play as your "personal train" when the game starts (example: 12-5, 5-7, 7-8, 8-11, 11-1, 1-9, and so on). When you are no longer able to line up your tiles in a matching series, the leftover tiles are considered your "extras" and will be used on the "Mexican Train" or on other players' "personal trains" during the game. If you do not

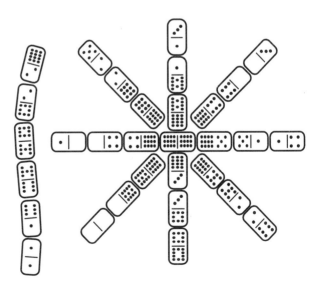

draw a domino with an end that matches the engine/centerpiece tile, you can begin the line in your hand with any domino that will make up the longest line of end-matching tiles and the fewest "extras" possible.

To begin the game, choose a player at random to play first and then rotate the starters clockwise thereafter.

The first player must begin by either playing a matching tile from the "line-up" in his hand onto the engine/centerpiece nearest him, so beginning his "personal train," or by playing one of his "extra" dominoes to be the first of the Mexican Train. This Mexican Train is a line of "end-matching" dominoes that can run around the edge of the table or at some side space convenient to all players. The Mexican Train, one's own "personal train," and other player's "personal trains" (when markered) are the options that players can use to rid themselves of their tiles.

The Mexican Train begins with the first tile played by the player who chooses to play a domino from his "extras." It must be a domino whose end is the same as the engine/centerpiece. The train then grows as others play on it, but it can only be played on from the tail end, opposite the end that matches the engine's pips. The "personal trains" are spokes that grow outward from the engine/centerpiece and appear as spokes on a hub. Wooden or plastic hubs

are available to conveniently hold the engine and the "personal trains." The number of spokes or "personal trains" coming from the engine are determined by the number of players participating. Spokes can be squeezed in, if more than 8 players are involved, or if Double-15s are used.

It is always wise to start the Mexican Train as soon as possible as it gives more places to play. Try to play your "extra" tiles on the Mexican Train before you play on your "personal train."

After the starter has played one domino, the next player to the left does likewise by playing on the Mexican Train, beginning his own "personal train" leading off from the engine, or playing on another player's "personal train" if it has a marker on it. When a player cannot play on his own "personal train," or on the Mexican Train, or on another player's train, he must draw one tile and try to play it immediately. If unable to do so, the player passes and must put his marker out on the last tile in his "personal train" (even if it has not been started), marking it so that the last number to be matched shows clearly to everyone. Others can play indefinitely on that markered train until the "owner" plays on it and removes the marker.

If a player plays a double during play, it is placed sideways and he must then play a second domino somewhere on the table. He does not necessarily need to play on the double he has just played. If he cannot play a second domino, he must draw another tile, then either play it or place his marker on his personal train.

After a double is played, all play is delayed until someone can make a play on this double. It doesn't matter if the next player can play somewhere else or not. He must play a tile on the double tile, even if he has to play a tile out of his train line-up in his hand. (This is disrupting, but necessary.) If players cannot play a tile on the double tile, they must draw once. If they are still unable to play a tile on the double, they pass and must place their marker on their "personal train" even if they had a matching tile to play on their train before the double was played. This means that once a tile has been played on the double tile, anyone can play on any "personal train" that has a marker on it, although this can *really* disrupt that train for the owner.

A player can play two doubles, as long as that player is able to play an additional tile from his hand (he is not allowed to draw) on one of those double tiles. This means that a player could play 3 tiles in one turn.

Play then proceeds to the left. When any player is left with just one tile in his hand, he must give notice to the other players by tapping his final tile on the table. This allows other players a chance to lower their score by ridding themselves of a higher numbered tile on their next turn.

General rules: If a player has a tile in his hand that will play, he must play that tile. He may not draw another.

If there are no more tiles in the bonepile, a player must pass if he does not hold a playable tile.

It is possible for a game to end by playing a double alone and no one being able to play on it.

The game is over when one player has dominoed (played his final tile) or when the game is blocked because no one holds a playable tile. Then, all players must count the number of pips on the tiles left in their hands (0, in the case of the player who has dominoed), and give that number—their score—to the scorekeeper.

As soon as the first round is completed, the next game begins by pulling out the 11-11, if playing with a double-12 set, or the 8-8, if playing with a double-9 set. The starter tile is placed in the middle of the table for the engine, and the rest of the deck is shuffled before drawing hands. All "personal trains" and the Mexican Train must be started with this same numbered new tile. Each new game thereafter should begin with the next-lowest double being played as the engine, with the 0-0 tile being the final engine for the last game.

The player with the lowest total score after all the games have been played is the winner.

Stretch

What's unique: At the end of each hand, all players count the total number of pips on the tiles, if any, remaining in their hand. That number is then subtracted from their own score, unlike in most games where that number would be added to the winner's score.

Playing with this variation does lengthen the game. Hence, the appropriate name—Stretch.

Use the rules to Block, Draw, Muggins, or many other games, with this exception:

At the end of each hand, players count the total number of pips on the tiles, if any, remaining in their hand and that number is then subtracted from their own score.

Latin American Match Dominoes

What's unique: Each hand that is won counts as one game, and a match ends when a team has won at least 10 games.
Domino set: Double-6.

Play this game using the rules to Block with these variations:
Number of players: 4 players play as 2 teams of 2 players per team.
Set: Player holding the 6-6 makes the first play with that tile.

Although each hand that is won counts as one game, and a match ends when one team has won at least 10 games, a match win is scored only if the other team failed to win 5 games. In which case, the match is considered to end with a tie.

Cuban Dominoes

Block game with these exceptions:
Domino set: Played with double-9.
Number of dominoes drawn: 4 players draw 10 tiles each. The remaining 15 tiles stay in the boneyard and are not drawn.
Set: Highest double starts play. After the set, play continues to the right (counterclockwise).

Doubles

What's unique: Before playing any tile from your hand, there must already be a double in the layout of the same suit as the matching end of the tile you wish to play.

This game is played using the rules to Draw with the following exceptions:
Set: The player who is holding the heaviest double leads with that tile. The set double is a spinner. Before you can play any tile from your hand, there must already be a double in the layout of the same suit as the matching end of the tile that you wish to play.

Here is an example, a player wishes to play the 3-4 tile in his or her hand by matching the 3 end to another tile in the layout with an exposed end of 3. A player can only do this if the 3-3 has already been played and is, therefore, in the layout. There does not have to be a 4-4 in the layout because the other end of the 3-4 tile the player wishes to play (the 4 end) is not the end of the tile that is being matched in that particular play.

Tiddle-a-Wink

(aka Tiddly-Wink)

What's unique: After you play a double, you have the option to play another tile (the Block game with this one exception).

Number of players: 2 or more.

Excellent party game for 3 to 6 individual players. May also be played by teams.

Domino Pool

What's unique: The game is played with a pool.

This is the Block game with these exceptions:

Number of players: 2 or more. Excellent party game for 3 to 6 individual players. May also be played by teams.

Number of dominoes drawn: Divide the tiles between the players, leaving at least 8 dominoes in the boneyard. For example: If 3 players, draw 6 tiles; 4 players, draw 5; 5 players, draw 4; 6 players, draw 3.

Set: Draw lots to determine who makes the first play. Any domino can be set.Before the game begins, each player puts an equal, agreed-upon, amount of money (or number of chips, dried beans, etc.) into the pool. And, once the pool has been won, each player puts an equal, agreed-upon, amount of money into the pool again before beginning the next game.

Scoring: The winner of the hand gets the pool. The winner of the hand is 1) the first player to domino; or 2) the player with the smallest count left in his hand, if the game ends in a block. In the event the low count is tied in a game ending in a block, the pool is divided among the low hands.

Variation: The first player or team to reach 100 points wins the pool.

Matador

(aka Master Dominoes, Seven-Up, Russian Dominoes, Russian Cross, and All Sevens.

What's unique: The sum of the tiles touching sides in the layout must total 7. (This is the Block game with this one exception.)

Blind Dominoes

(aka Blind Hughie, Secret Dominoes, Blind-Man Block, and Billiton.

It's obvious why the game goes by the names of Blind or Secret Dominoes: Players don't know what tiles they hold in their hand and are unable to choose their play. But what about the name Billiton? The word is the anglicized spelling of Belitung, an island off the former Dutch colony of Sumatra, so maybe this game was a pastime of the Dutch colonists or was an Oriental import.

What's unique: A player doesn't see his hand until he plays it.

Number of players: 2 to 4 players

Number of dominoes drawn: 2 players, draw 14; 3 players, draw 9; 4 players, draw 7. The entire deck is drawn, except with 3 players, when the one undrawn tile is set.

Variation: 2 players, draw 8; 3 players, draw 7; 4 players, draw 6. Remaining tiles are discarded.

Set: Draw lots to determine who makes the first play.

How to play: Each player draws his tiles from the boneyard without looking at the face of the domino. Keeping the tiles facedown on the table, each player arranges his tiles 1) in a vertical row, long side to long side, playing his tiles one at a time from the top of his row or from the bottom of his row; or 2) in a horizontal row, long side to long side, playing tiles from his row in any order he chooses. Players should decide at the beginning of the game whether to they want to play from top to bottom, bottom to top, or in any order the players choose.

Let's say the players have decided to play from top to bottom, and Mark is the first player. Mark turns over his first tile, the tile on the top of his vertical row. Then he turns over a second tile, the next tile in his row. If he is able to play his second tile on his first tile by matching suits, he does so. He continues to turn over tiles as long as he is able to make a play. And, if he turns over a tile that can be played on more than one end of the line of play, he may turn over and look at the next tile in his row before choosing where to play his

domino. If he turns over a tile that he is unable to play, he places it facedown at the bottom of his row. If the tile Mark turned over and was unable to play happens to be a double, he places it faceup at the bottom of his row. Then, play continues with the next player, the one at Mark's left.

Variations: 1) During his turn, a player may choose to play any exposed double in his row. 2) A player's turn does not continue as long as he can make a play. Instead, a player is only allowed to turn over one tile per turn. 3) If playing the variation of turning over any tile of your choosing from your row (as opposed to playing from top to bottom or from bottom to top), when an unplayable tile is exposed during your turn, that tile is turned facedown and placed on the left end of your horizontal row.

Other rules:

- There are no spinners. (Variation: Only the first double played is a spinner.)
- Game ends when one player dominoes or when the game is blocked.

Tip: If playing the variation of turning over any tile of your choosing from your row (as opposed to playing from top to bottom or from bottom to top), it is certainly a help to the player's game if he can remember the position of the previously exposed tiles and therefore be able to turn them over during his turn when there is an open end in the line of play with a matching suit to the tile in his hand.

Cross Dominoes

(aka simply Cross)

What's unique: The first double played is a spinner and it must be played on both ends and both sides, forming a 5-tile cross, before any other tile can be played.

Variation: If after the first round of play not all four sides of the first double have been played upon, in subsequent rounds no tile can be played on the remaining open end (or ends) of the first double played.

Number of dominoes drawn: 2 play-ers, draw 7; 3 players, draw 6; 4 players, draw 5.

Variation: Each player draws 6 tiles and the remaining tiles are discarded. In this game variation, if

you cannot make a play, you must pass.

Set: The player holding the highest double makes the first play.

Other rules:

- Only the first double played is a spinner.
- A player may not pass if he is holding a playable tile in his hand.
- If a player cannot make a play, he must draw from the boneyard until he draws a playable domino. Do not draw the last two remaining dominoes in the boneyard.
- If a player cannot make a play, he must pass if 1) he was unable to draw a playable domino; 2) there are only two dominoes left in the boneyard, and therefore no more dominoes left to be drawn; or 3) playing the variation mentioned above, in which all players draw 6 tiles each and then must pass if a play cannot be made.
- Game ends when a player dominoes or when game is blocked.

Variation: The player who makes the first play by setting the highest double has the option to immediately add another tile to the set tile or to pass.

Cyprus

What's unique: The highest double is played as set. The set domino must be played on both ends, both sides, and diagonally, forming a 7-tile star with a double-6 set of dominoes or a 9-tile star with a double-9 or double-12 set, before any other tile can be played.

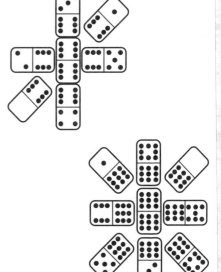

This is the Block game with the above and the set exception.

Set: The player holding the highest double begins play.

Maltese Cross

(aka Double Cross)

What's unique: The highest double is played as set. The set domino must be played on both ends and both sides, forming a 5-tile cross, before any other tile can be played.

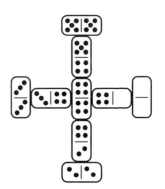

Next, a double must be played on each of the four tiles that are played from the set double before play continues with the rules to Block.

This is the Block game with the above and the set exception.

Set: The player holding the highest double begins play.

Sebastopol

(aka Malakoff)

What's unique: The 6-6 is played as set. The 6-6 is a spinner and must be played on both ends and both sides, forming a 5-tile cross, before any other tile can be played.

This is the Block game with the above and the set exception.

Set: The player who is holding the 6-6 domino begins play.

The Fortress

What's unique: This game is played with a double-9 set of dominoes; the double-9 is set domino; and 8 dominoes from the 9 suit must be played on the double-9 domino before any other tiles can be played.

Number of players: Best with 6 players; may be played with 4.

Number of dominoes drawn: 6 players, draw 9; 4 players, draw 13. If 6 are playing, the player to set the double-9 gets the remaining tile in the boneyard and plays again before the second player makes his play. If 4 are playing, the player to set the double-9 gets 1 of the 3 remaining tiles in the boneyard and plays again before the second player makes his play.

Variation: 6 players, draw 7; 4 players, draw 9.

Set: Double-9.

Other rules: If the double-9 tile is in the boneyard because it was not drawn when players drew their hands, let the player who lost the last hand draw from the boneyard and then set the double-9 tile.

No spinners except the set domino, double-9, which is played on 8 sides.

Game score can be 100, 150, or 200 points.

Chickenfoot®

(© 1987 by Louis and Betty Howsley)

Domino set: Double-9 set
Number of players: 2 and up

This is the game of Draw with these exceptions:

What's unique: Two different formations are made: the double chickenfoot and the chickenfoot. The double chickenfoot is made at the beginning of each hand by playing 6 tiles diagonally, 3 on each side, of the set tile. Chickenfoots are made throughout the hand by playing 3 tiles diagonally on one side of a double played during the game. Tiles played diagonally on the double tile are called "chickentoes." A chickenfoot or a double chickenfoot must have all the chickentoes before any other plays can be made.

Also unique: 50 points are added to your score at the end of a hand if you are left holding the 0-0 tile.

Object of the game: To be the player with the lowest score at the end of the game.

Number of tiles drawn: Each player draws an equal number of tiles from the "chicken yard." For example: If 2 play, each draws 20 tiles; if 8 play, each draws 6 tiles. There are 55 tiles in the set. Tiles left after each player draws remain in the chicken yard to be drawn from during the hand.

Set: Player holding the 9-9 makes the first play of the game. Subsequent games would begin with the next-lowest double tile (8-8; 7-7; 6-6; and so on, the last game beginning with the 0-0 tile). If no one holds the correct double tile to begin that particular hand, players may agree to either 1) go to the next-lowest double (for example, 8-8 in the case of the first play of the game) or 2) reshuffle all the tiles and draw new hands. Play continues to the left.

The next 6 plays must be made on the 9-9 tile, 3 tiles played diagonally on each side of the 9-9 tile. This formation is called a "double chickenfoot." To do this, players must match a tile from their hand of the 9 suit to the 9-9 set tile.

If 6 tiles have not been played on the 9-9 set and a player does not hold a tile from the 9 suit in his hand, he may draw one tile from the chicken yard. If he draws a tile with a 9 end, he plays it on the set tile. If he does not draw a tile from the 9 suit, he must pass his turn to the player on his left.

After 6 tiles have been played on the 9-9 set tile, plays can be made on any of the 6 "chickentoes" by matching tiles end to end, until someone plays a double tile.

Once a double tile has been played on one of the chickentoes, the next three plays must be made on the double tile before plays can be made anywhere else in the layout. This formation of 3 tiles played on the double tile is called a chickenfoot.

Once the new chickenfoot has been completed by playing 3 tiles

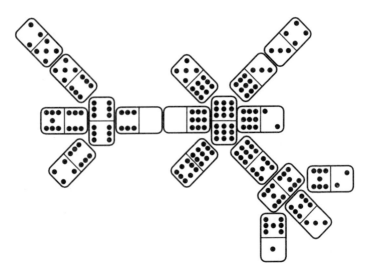

diagonally on one side of a double tile, players may return to adding tiles to any of the chicken toes until someone plays another double.

The game ends once a player plays all the tiles in his hand or when the game ends in block because none of the players are able to make a play and there are no tiles in the chicken yard to draw from. Players must count the dots on the tiles remaining in their hand (1 point per 1 dot) and record their score. Remember, the player caught having the 0-0 gets 50 points.

For the next hand, tiles are reshuffled and each player draws the same number of tiles from the chicken yard as he or she did at the beginning of the previous hand played. The second hand begins with the 8-8 tile; the third hand, with the 7-7 tile; and so on.

For a longer game, players may choose to continue playing by starting another hand with the 1-1 tile following the hand that began with the 0-0 tile as set. Subsequent hands would begin with the next-highest double played as set (2-2; 3-3; and so on, up to the last hand beginning with the 9-9 tile).

Fours

What's unique: This game is for four players only and each must play individually and not as a team. Also, players can continue to play as long as they can make a match.
How to play: Play by the rules to Block with these exceptions.

Number of players: 4 players, each playing individually, no teams. The first player is determined by lot.

Anytime a player makes a play, he may continue to play as long as he can make a match.

Add-'Em-Up 50

What's unique: When a player plays a tile that matches an open end in the line of play, the number of pips on the tile's open end is added to his score, and the first player to reach 50 or more points is the winner and yells, "Domino!"
Number of dominoes drawn: Each player draws 5 tiles
Set: Any tile may be set and is set by the last person to draw from the boneyard

If the first player sets a double, he earns points of the total number of pips on that tile; if it is a single, he earns points of the total number of pips on the heaviest end of the tile. Play then continues to his left.

The next player makes a play by matching one of the ends of the set tile with one of the ends of a tile from his hand. This player earns points of the total number of pips on the exposed end of his tile (the end that does not match the set tile). Play continues, clockwise around the table, in this manner.

Any time a player is unable to make a play, he must draw from the boneyard until he draws a playable tile. A player must pass if there are no tiles left in the boneyard and he holds no playable tile in his hand.

The first player to reach 50 or more points is the winner and gets to shout, "Domino!"

Variations: You may change the number of points a player must receive in order to win the game. To shorten or lengthen the game, make the number of points to win lower or higher than 50 points. In the case of a longer game: If all tiles in the deck have been played before any player reaches the winning score, start a new game, but add points earned to your score from the previous game(s).

Pass

What's unique: A player has the option of passing up his turn and not making a play even when he holds a playable tile in his hand and/or there are still available tiles in the boneyard. (Play by the rules for Draw with this one exception.)

One-Arm Joe

What's unique: Plays can only be made on one side of the set tile.

Number of players: Any number, however 5 to 9 players is best. Those playing may chose to play in teams of two, three, or four per team.

Object of the game: To be the first to domino.

Number of dominoes drawn: Each player draws 3 tiles.

Set: Player with highest double.

Any time a player makes a play on a double, including the set double, he may play a second tile before his turn is up.

When a player cannot make a play, he or she should draw from the boneyard until drawing a playable tile. If there are no tiles left in the boneyard to draw from and the player has no playable tile in his hand, he must pass.

The first player to play all tiles in his hand announces, "Domino!"

If a game ends in a block, all the players turn their dominoes face-up, count the pips on each tile, and add the numbers together. The player who dominoed, or the player with the lowest total if the game ended in a block, wins the game and gets the points of all the other players.

The player who gets 100 points or more first is the overall winner.

Scoring Games

All the games in this section are called scoring games because scoring is done during play and at the end of each hand.

In these several games, a player is awarded points every time he makes a play that results in the open ends of the tiles in the line of play adding up to a multiple of 5: Muggins, All Fives, Five-Up, Sniff, Seven-Toed Pete, and Merry-Go-Round.

In the game of All Threes, points are awarded to a player when he makes a play that results in the open ends of the tiles in the line of play adding up to a multiple of 3; and, in the game of Threes and Fives, points are awarded for multiples of 3 and multiples of 5.

In the game of Bergen, points are scored by a player after he makes a play resulting in both open ends of the tiles in the line of play being alike.

All the games in this section, with the exception of Bergen, are very similar. And, just like most of the domino games in this book, sometimes the identical game rules go by two or more different names depending on what country or what part of a country you are in. Sometimes games that go by the same name aren't played with the same rules. Then there are also many, many different variations of certain games that go by a slightly different, but very similar, name.

Here are some examples of what I found in my research.

Five different domino game instruction books state that what makes the game of All Fives unique from all other games in the "five-point family" of games is that when hands are drawn at the beginning of the game, only five tiles per player are drawn regardless of the number of players. Yet, in another book written by a group of authors most consider to be experts, players of the game of All Fives are instructed to draw 7 tiles each if there are 2 playing and 5 tiles each if there are 3 or 4 players.

The very thing that is said to make the game of Five-Up unique from all other games in the "five-point family" of games is that every double played is a spinner. Yet I found rules to the game in one place that make no mention at all that every double played is a spinner.

I could give many more such examples For this book, I have attempted to list variations of rules.When I found rules that contradict each other, as in the examples above, I went with the most-often-noted rules.

Unless otherwise indicated, the games here use the following rules:
- One set of double-6 dominoes (28 pieces) is used.
- Shuffle the dominoes, facedown, at the beginning of each hand.
- *Object of the game:* To gain the highest score possible by making points while playing the game and by being the first player to domino.

Muggins

What's unique: If a player should overlook a score, his opponent may call "Muggins!" and take the score himself.

Number of players: 2 to 4 players. The game may be played in partnership when there are 4 players.

Number of dominoes drawn: If 2 play, each player draws 7 tiles. If 3 or 4 play, each player draws 5 tiles.

Variations: 1) No more than 4 can play, and every player, regardless of the number of players, draws 7 tiles. 2) If 4 play, each draws 5 tiles; if 3 play, each draws 6; and, if 2 play, each draws 7.

The tiles not drawn are pushed to one side to make up the boneyard.

Set: Lots are drawn to determine who sets the first tile. The first player may play any domino in his hand. After the first tile has been set, play continues to the left.

Variation: The player holding the highest double in his hand makes the first play by setting that tile. After the first tile has been set, play continues to the left.

The first double played is a spinner.

Variation: There are no spinners.

How to Play: After the first domino is set, subsequent players must join a tile from their hand with an open end in the line of play. The ends of the two tiles that are joined must have the same number of pips.

If a player is unable to make a play from his hand, he must draw tiles from the boneyard until he draws a playable tile. If a player is unable to make a play from his hand and there are no tiles left in the boneyard, the player must skip his turn until he is able to make a play.

Variations: 1) When there are 2 players, the last two tiles in the boneyard may not be drawn. If there are 3 or 4 players, the last tile in the boneyard may not be drawn. 2) If a player has a playable tile, he must play it. 3) A player may draw from the boneyard even if he holds a playable tile in his hand.

Scoring: A player is awarded points every time he makes a play that results in the open ends of the tiles in the line of play adding up to a multiple of 5. (5 points for 5 pips; 10 points for 10 pips; 15 points for 15 pips; and so on.) Each player must announce his points on making his play in order to receive credit for the points made. If a player overlooks a score, his opponent may call, "Muggins!" and take the score himself.

The player who dominoes is also awarded points at the end of each hand by adding up, and rounding to the nearest multiple of 5, the pips on the tiles left in his opponents' hands. 1 or 2 pips is worth nothing; 3, 4, 5, 6, and 7 is worth 5 points; 8, 9, 10, 11, and 12 is worth 10 points; and so on. The first player, or partnership if 4 are playing, to reach 200 points wins the game. If a player reaches 200 points during play, the game ends at that point. If points are tallied at the end of a hand and more than one player has a score of 200 or more, the player with the highest score wins. In case of a tie, follow these rules: If 2 are playing, play two more hands; 3 players, play three more hands; 4 players, play four more hands.

Variations: 1) The first to reach 100 points wins the game. 2) A player is awarded one point every time he makes a play that results in the open ends of the tiles in the line of play adding up to a multiple of 5. (1 point for 5 pips; 2 points for 10 pips; 3 points for 15 pips; and so on.) The player who dominoes is also awarded points— one point for each multiple of 5— at the end of each hand by adding up, and rounding to the nearest multiple of 5, the pips on the tiles left in his opponents' hands. The first player, or partnership if 4 are playing, to reach exactly 61 points wins the game. If any play made causes the player's or partnership's total score to exceed 61 points, then no points at all are scored for that particular play, and play continues to the left. 3) If a larger group is playing, players may wish to reduce the number of points that must be reached in order to win the game. The number of points to be reached must be agreed upon by all the players prior to the start of the game.

Scoring if hand is blocked: Each player counts the pips on the remaining tiles in his hand. The player with the lowest number of pips scores the difference between his total and that of each of his opponents. Then, the player with the next-lowest number of pips scores the difference between his total and that of each of his opponents, and so on.

Variations: 1) The player with the lowest number of pips scores the total number of pips in his opponent's hand. If there is a tie for the lowest number of pips, there is no score. 2) The player with the lowest number of pips wins the game.

Scoring when partners play: Players must play individually, but a common score is kept for partners. When one player dominoes, the number of pips on the tiles remaining in the hand of his partner are subtracted from their score.

All Fives

What's unique: Players draw 5 tiles from the stock regardless of the number of players.

Number of players: 2 to 4 players. The game may be played in partnership when there are 4 players.

Number of dominoes drawn: Players draw 5 tiles from the stock regardless of the number of players. The tiles not drawn are pushed to one side to make up the boneyard.

Set: Lots are drawn to determine who sets the first tile. The first player may play any domino in his hand. After the first tile has been set, play continues to the left. The first double played is a spinner.

How to play: After the first domino is set, subsequent players must join a tile from their hand with an open end in the line of play. The ends of the two tiles that are joined must have the same number of pips.

If a player is unable to make a play from his hand, he must draw tiles from the boneyard until he draws a playable tile. If a player is unable to make a play from his hand and there are no tiles left in the boneyard, the player must skip his turn until he is able to make a play.

Variations: 1) When there are 2 players, the last two tiles in the boneyard may not be drawn. If there are 3 or 4 players, the last tile in the boneyard may not be drawn. 2) If a player has a playable tile, he must play it. 3) If a player plays a tile that scores points or if a player plays a dou- ble, he plays another tile from his hand before the next player takes a turn. If he is unable to play anoth- er tile from his hand, he draws from the boneyard until he draws a playable tile or until the bone- yard is exhausted. 4) A player can- not "domino" with a scoring tile or a double. If he plays the last tile in his hand and it is a double or a scoring tile, he must draw from the boneyard until he draws a playable tile or until the boneyard is exhausted. If the boneyard is already exhausted at the time the player would play his last piece, he must skip his turn, and play con- tinues to the left.

Scoring: A player is awarded points every time he makes a play that results in the open ends of the tiles in the line of play adding up to a multiple of 5. (5 points for 5 pips; 10 points for 10 pips; 15 points for 15 pips; and so on.) The play- er who dominoes is also awarded points at the end of each hand by adding up, and rounding to the nearest multiple of 5, the pips on the tiles left in his opponents' hands. Only 1 or 2 pips is worth nothing; 3, 4, 5, 6, and 7 is worth 5 points; 8, 9, 10, 11, and 12 is worth 10 points; and so on. The first player, or partnership if 4 are playing, to reach 200 points wins the game. If a player reaches 200 points during play, the game ends at that point. If points are tallied at the end of a hand and more than one player has a score of 200 or more, the player with the highest score wins. In case of a tie, follow these rules: If 2 are playing, play two more hands; 3 players, play three more hands; 4 players, play four more hands.

Variations: 1) The first to reach 150 points wins the game. 2) First to reach 250 points wins the game. 3) A player is awarded one point every time he makes a play that results in the open ends of the tiles in the line of play adding up to a multiple of 5. (1 point for 5 pips; 2 points for 10 pips; 3 points for 15 pips; and so on.) The play- er who dominoes is also awarded points—one point for each multi- ple of 5—at the end of each hand by adding up, and rounding to the nearest multiple of 5, the pips on the tiles left in his opponents' hands. The first player, or partnership if 4 are playing, to reach exactly 61 points wins the game. If any play made causes the player's or partnership's total score to exceed 61 points, then no points at all are scored for that particular play and play continues to the left. 4) If a larger group is playing, players may wish to reduce the number of points that must be reached in order to win the game. The reduced number of points needed must be agreed upon by all the players prior to the start of the game. 5) The number of pips on the open end of a just-played tile may be subtracted from the total of the other ends of the layout, instead of being added, to make a multiple of five.

Scoring if hand is blocked: Each player counts the pips on the remaining tiles in his hand. The player with the lowest number of pips scores the difference between his total and that of each of his opponents. Then, the player with the next-lowest number of pips scores the difference between his total and that of each of his opponents, and so on.

Variations: The player with the lowest number of pips scores the total number of pips in his opponents' hands. If there is a tie for the lowest number of pips in a two-handed or four-handed game, there is no score. If there is a tie for the lowest number of pips in a three-handed game, the number of pips in their opponent's hand is split evenly between them.

Scoring when partners play: Players must play individually, but a common score is kept for partners. When a player dominoes, the number of pips on the tiles remaining in the hand of his partner are subtracted from their score.

Five-Up

(aka West Coast Dominoes in U.S.)

This game was created over fifty years ago in the San Francisco area, which has, since 1969, been headquarters to the International Domino Association (IDA). The game's popularity can be attributed to Dominic Armanino, the author of several domino game instruction books, including one devoted entirely to the game of Five-Up. Mr. Armanino was also a founder of the IDA, and Five-Up has always been the game played at IDA-sponsored tournaments.

What's unique: Every double played is a possible spinner.

Number of players: 2 to 4 players. The game may be played in partnership when there are 4 players.

Number of dominoes drawn: 5.
Variation: If 2 play, each player draws 7 tiles. If 3 or 4 play, each player draws 5 tiles.

The tiles not drawn are pushed to one side to make up the boneyard.

Set: Lots are drawn to determine who sets the first tile. The first player may play any domino in his hand. After the first tile has been set, play continues to the left. Every double played is a possible spinner.

How to play: After the first domino is set, subsequent players must join a tile from their hand with an open end in the line of play. The ends of the two tiles that are joined must have the same number of pips.

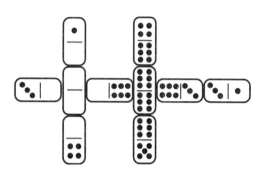

If a player is unable to make a play from his hand, he must draw tiles from the boneyard until he draws a playable tile. If a player is unable to make a play from his hand and there are no tiles left in the boneyard, the player must skip his turn until he is able to make a play.

Variations: 1) When there are 2 players, the last two tiles in the boneyard may not be drawn. If there are 3 or 4 players, the last tile in the boneyard may not be drawn. 2) If a player has a playable tile, he must play it.

Scoring: A player is awarded one point every time he makes a play that results in the open ends of the tiles in the line of play adding up to a multiple of 5. (1 point for 5 pips; 2 points for 10 pips; 3 points for 15 pips; and so on.) The player who dominoes is also awarded

points—one point for each multiple of 5—at the end of each hand by adding up, and rounding to the nearest multiple of 5, the pips on the tiles left in his opponents' hands. 1 or 2 pips is worth nothing; 3, 4, 5, 6, and 7 is worth 1 point; 8, 9, 10, 11, and 12 is worth 2 points, and so on. The first player, or partnership if 4 are playing, to reach exactly 61 points wins the game. If any play made causes the player's or partnership's total score to exceed 61 points, then no points at all are scored for that particular play, and play continues to the left.

Variation: If a larger group is playing, players may wish to reduce the number of points that must be reached in order to win the game. The number of points to be reached must be agreed upon by all the players prior to the start of the game.

Scoring if hand is blocked: Each player counts the pips on the remaining tiles in his or her hand. The player with the lowest number of pips scores the difference between his total and that of each of his opponents. Then the player with the next-lowest number of pips scores the difference between his total and that of each of his opponents, and so on.

Variations: The player with the lowest number of pips scores the total number of pips in his opponent's hand. If there is a tie for the lowest number of pips in a two-handed or four-handed game, there is no score. If there is a tie for the lowest number of pips in a three-handed game, the number of pips in their opponent's hand is split evenly between them.

Scoring when partners play: Players must play individually, but a common score is kept for partners. When one player dominoes, the number of pips on the tiles remaining in the hand of his partner are subtracted from their score.

Sniff

(aka as East Coast Dominoes in U.S. and Partnership Dominoes)

What's unique: The first, and only the first, domino played is a spinner, or "sniff." The pips on any open end of the sniff are counted for points until plays have been made on all four ends.

Number of players: 2 to 4 players; the game may be played in partnership when there are 4 players.

Number of dominoes drawn: If 2 play, each player draws 7 tiles. If 3 or 4 play, each player draws 5 tiles.

Variations: 1) No more than 4 can play and every player draws 7 tiles. 2) If 4 play, each draws 5 tiles; if 3 play, each draws 6; and, if 2 play, each draws 7.

The tiles not drawn are pushed to one side to make up the boneyard.

Set: Lots are drawn to determine who sets the first tile. The first player may play any domino in his hand. After the first tile has been set, play continues to the left.

Variation: The player holding the highest double in his hand makes the first play by setting that tile. After the first tile has been set, play continues to the left.

The first double played is a spinner.

Scoring: A player is awarded points every time he makes a play that results in the open ends of the tiles in the line of play adding up to a multiple of 5. (5 points for 5 pips; 10 points for 10 pips; 15 points for 15 pips; and so on.) The player who dominoes is also awarded points at the end of each hand by adding up, and rounding to the nearest multiple of 5, the pips on the tiles left in his opponents' hands. 1 or 2 pips is worth nothing; 3, 4, 5, 6, and 7 is worth 1 point; 8, 9, 10, 11, and 12 is worth 2 points, and so on. The first player, or partnership if 4 are playing, to reach 200 points wins the game.

Variations: 1) First to reach 100 points wins the game. 2) A player is awarded one point every time he makes a play that results in the open ends of the tiles in the line of play adding up to a multiple of 5. (1 point for 5 pips; 2 points for 10 pips; 3 points for 15 pips; and so on.) The player who dominoes is also awarded points—one point for each multiple of 5—at the end of each hand by adding up, and rounding to the nearest multiple of 5, the pips on the tiles left in his opponents' hands. The first player, or partnership if 4 are playing, to reach exactly 61 points wins the game. If any play made causes the player's or partnership's total score to exceed 61 points, then no points at all are scored for that particular play and play continues to the left. 3) If a larger group is playing, players may wish to reduce the number of points that must be reached in order to win the game. The number of points to be reached must be agreed upon by all the players prior to the start of the game.

All Threes

What's unique: A player is awarded points every time he makes a play that results in the open ends of the tiles in the line of play adding up to a multiple of 3.
Number of players: 2 to 4 players. 4 players may play as two teams of 2 players per team.

The tiles not drawn are pushed to one side to make up the boneyard.
Set: Lots are drawn to determine who sets the first tile. The first player may play any domino in his hand. After the first tile has been set, play continues to the left. The first double played is a spinner.
Scoring: A player is awarded points every time he makes a play that

results in the open ends of the tiles in the line of play adding up to a multiple of 3. (3 points for 3 pips; 6 points for 6 pips; 9 points for 9 pips; and so on.) The player who dominoes is also awarded points at the end of each hand by adding up, and rounding to the nearest multiple of 3, the pips on the tiles left in his opponents' hands. 1 pip is worth nothing; 2, 3, and 4 is worth 3 points; 5, 6, and 7 is worth 6 points; and so on. The first player, or partnership if 4 are playing, to reach 200 points wins the game.

Variations: 1) The first player to reach 150 points wins the game. 2) First to reach 250 points wins the game. 3) A player is awarded one point every time he makes a play that results in the open ends of the tiles in the line of play adding up to a multiple of 3. (1 point for 3 pips; 2 points for 6 pips; 3 points for 9 pips; and so on.) The player who dominoes is also awarded points—one point for each multiple of 3—at the end of each hand by adding up, and rounding to the nearest multiple of 3, the pips on the tiles left in his opponents' hands. The first player, or partnership if 4 are playing, to reach exactly 61 points wins the game. If any play made causes the player's or partnership's total score to exceed 61 points, then no points at all are scored for that particular play, and play continues to the left. 4) If a larger group is playing, players may wish to reduce the number of points that must be reached in order to win the game. The number of points to be reached must be agreed upon by all the players prior to the start of the game.

Seven-Toed Pete

(aka Racehorse and Seven Go)

What's unique: If a player plays a double or one of the 5 scoring dominoes (6-4, 5-5, 5-0, 4-1, or 3-2), he may continue to play tiles from his hand.

Object of the game: To make the total count of the exposed ends of tiles played equal 5 or a multiple of 5.

This is the same game as Five-Up, but with three variations.

Number of players: 2 to 4 players. 4 players may play as two teams of 2 players per team.

Number of dominoes drawn: 7 tiles per player.

Set: First player must play a double tile or a score tile. If the first player is unable to play a double tile or a score tile to set, he 1) passes if there are 4 players, or 2) draws from the boneyard if there are 2 or 3 players.

Scoring: 1 point for every multiple of 5. For example: A total of 5 pips on the exposed ends of the tiles in the layout is worth 1 point; 10 pips is worth 2 points; 15 pips, 3 points.

When a player plays a double or a score tile, including the set domino, he must play again.

A player may play any matching tile in his hand to the set domino. If he scores or plays a double, he must make another play or 1) pass if there are 4 players, or 2) draw from the boneyard until he draws a playable tile if there are 2 or 3 players.

In a game of 2 or 3 players, if a player's last tile is a double or a score tile, he must play it and then draw from the boneyard until he draws another playable tile. In the case of a 2-handed game, he must leave 2 tiles in the boneyard; in a 3-handed game, 1 tile. If he does not hold a playable tile and there are no more available tiles in the boneyard, he must pass. Play continues until 1 player has played the last tile in his hand, and it is not a double tile or a score tile.

In a game of 4 players, if a player's last tile is a double or a score tile, he is "washed up." The other players continue to play until 1 player has played the last tile in his hand, and it is not a double tile or a score tile.

The game is over when 1 player dominoes or when the game is blocked. The player or team with the lowest number of pips left in his hand (0 in the case of a player who has dominoed) is the winner and receives 1 point for every pip left on the remaining tiles in his opponents' hands.

Threes and Fives

What's unique: A player is awarded points every time he makes a play that results in the open ends of the tiles in the line of play adding up to a multiple of 3 or a multiple of 5.

Play by the rules of Muggins, with these exceptions.

A player scores 1 point per pip when the total number of pips on the exposed ends of the tiles in the layout is a multiple of 3 or a multiple of 5. If, after making a play, the total number of pips on the exposed ends of the tiles in the layout total 10, which is a multiple of 5, that player would score 10 points. If the total number of pips was 12, which is a multiple of 3, that player would score 12 points. If the total number of pips was 30, a multiple of 3 and a multiple of 5, that player would score 60 points (30+30).

The game is over when one player has dominoed or when the game is blocked. Once the game is over, each player should count the total number of pips on the remaining tiles in his hand. The player who dominoed or the player left with the lowest number of pips in his hand at the end of the game is the winner. The winner earns a score of the total number of pips left in his opponents' hands (1 point per 1 pip).

The game is usually 251 points.

Merry-Go-Round

What's unique: A double must be set and the succeeding plays must be made on both sides, first, and then on both ends of the set tile, until all four sides have been played on.
Number of players: 2 to 4 players.
Number of dominoes drawn: Each player draws 7 tiles.
Set: The first player must set a double. If he does not hold a double in his hand, he must draw from the boneyard until he draws a double and then use that double to make his first play.

After a tile has been played on each of the four sides of the set domino, plays may be made on any exposed end, in any order, with a single or a double tile.

Play by the rules to Five-Up with the above exceptions.

Bergen

(aka Double-Header)

Bergen is German for mountains. Because the game is sometimes referred to as "the Bergen game," there is reason to believe it did not originate in Germany, but might have come instead from Bergen op Zoom, a coastal town in the Netherlands, or from Bergen, Norway. *What's unique:* Both open ends of the layout must be made alike. *Number of players:* 2 to 4.

Same as for the Block game or Muggins, with the following exceptions:

Number of dominoes drawn: Each player draws 6 tiles.

You *must* make both open ends of the layout alike.

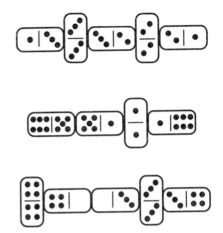

Trump and Trick Games

The games in this section are very different from those games categorized as "blocking" and "scoring" games. Tiles are *not* matched on the table to form a layout. Instead, they are ranked by suit; trumps are named; tricks are taken; and in all but one game in this section, players bid on their hand.

The most popular of all the what I call "trump and trick" games is the game of Forty-Two. Numerous bidding variations for the game of Forty-Two have been created—to name a few: Big Bertha; Cajun Hokey Pokey; Eagle Eye; East Lansing Deferred-Style Nillo; Follow Me; Inverted Low Boy; Low; Low Boy; Multiple Trumps Forty-Two; Naperville Onesies; Near-Seven; No Catchem; No Trump; Splash; and West Texas Rules. In this section, I will give a brief description of three bidding variations: Sevens, Plunge, and Nel-O (sometimes spelled Nillo).

Unless otherwise indicated: one set of double-6 dominoes (28 pieces) is used.

The dominoes are shuffled, facedown, at the beginning of each hand.

Forty-Two

(aka Texas Forty-Two, Four-Hand Texas, and Domino Rounce)

Forty-Two is an adaptation of Auction Pitch. It was invented by W. A. Thomas during his boyhood in Garner, Parker County, Texas, about 1885; then it spread throughout the southwestern United States.

In this game, if a team collects each of the 7 tricks (1 point per trick) and each of the 5-count dominoes (2 tiles worth 10 points each and 3 tiles worth 5 points each, for a total of 35 points) in the course of one hand, he will have a total of 42 points (7+35 = 42). Thus, the name of the game.

Object of the game: To be the first team to reach 250 points.

Number of players: 4 players play as 2 teams of 2 players per team.

Draw lots at the beginning of the game to determine which player shuffles first. Reshuffle the tiles. *Number of dominoes drawn:* Each player draws 7 tiles. All players, except for the shuffler, simultaneously draw 7 tiles from the deck. The shuffler, then, draws the 7 remaining tiles.

The person to the shuffler's left has the first option to bid.

Your bid is a prediction of how many of the 42 points you will win in that hand. Your bid should be based almost entirely on your own hand. However, if you win the bid, any points won by your partner during that hand

will also count towards your bid.

If you hold at least 3 tiles from the same suit in your hand, that is considered a potential bidding hand. That suit will be your trump suit if you win the bid. If you hold 1 or 2 doubles in addition to 3 tiles from the same suit, this is considered a strong hand.

The word "trump" comes from the word "triumph." A domino from the trump suit automatically "triumphs" over other dominoes played. Once trumps for the hand have been declared, all 7 dominoes of that suit rank higher than all 21 other dominoes. Regardless of who plays it, the highest trump played wins any trick. A trump domino only belongs to the trump suit and not also to the other suit represented on its face. The other number on the trump domino only serves to rank trumps among themselves.

For example: If fours are trumps, the 4-4 is the strongest domino of the hand; the 4-6 beats the 4-5; the 4-5 beats the 4-3; and so on, the 4-0 being the lowest trump. The 4-0 for that hand would beat any tile that is not from the 4 suit.

The double is the highest domino of each suit, followed in order by the 6, 5, 4, 3, 2, 1, and blank.

A domino whose ends add up to five or a multiple of five is a "count" domino. There are two count tiles worth 10 points each: 5-5 and 6-4. There are three count tiles worth 5 points each: 5-0, 4-1, and 3-2. All 5-count tiles add up to a total of 35 points. A count scores extra points for the team that wins it in a trick.

Bidding continues clockwise around the table, with the shuffler always having the last option to bid. Each player has only one opportunity to bid. The minimum bid is 30. A player must pass if he is unable to bid at least 30 or raise a previous bid. If all 4 players pass, all tiles are returned to the deck and then reshuffled by the player to the left of the last player to shuffle.

The player making the highest bid is the first player and the player to declare which suit is trump for that hand. (A player never reveals the trump suit until he has won the bid and is ready to play the first tile.)

The first player plays a tile from his hand. Play continues to his left. The next three plays made by the other players at the table must "follow suit." This means those three players must play a tile that is of the same suit as the highest end of the first tile played in that trick, unless the first player plays a tile with at least one end from the same suit as what was declared "trumps" for that hand. In that case, the next three plays made must be a tile with an end from the trump suit.

For example, if the 6-4 is played first, the other players would have to follow suit with a 6 from their own hand. But if either end of the first tile played is of the trump suit, then the trump overrides the other number and everyone must follow suit with a trump.

If a player holds more than one playable tile in his hand, he may play any one of them. If a player is unable to follow suit because he does not hold that suit in his hand, he may play any tile from his hand, even a trump.

The player who plays the highest tile of the lead suit or the highest trump wins the trick. The winner of each trick plays the first tile for the next trick, at which time he may play any tile in his hand.

When all four players have each played one tile, these four tiles are collectively a trick. There are seven tricks in each hand. Each trick is worth one point.

One player from each team should collect all the tricks for that team, regardless of which player won the trick. After each trick has been won, the tiles should be moved to one side or corner of the table, the 4 tiles side by side and faceup. This simplifies scoring.

Once all 7 tricks have been played, each team should total their number of tricks (1 point per trick) and their total number of points on count dominoes collected (5 and multiples of 5), respectively.

If the bidding team makes or exceeds their bid, then that team receives credit for all the points they won during that hand. In that case, the opponents also receive credit for any points they won during the hand.

For example: If a team bids 30 and then takes 35 points in the hand, then it has successfully reached its bid and scores 35 points. The opponents receive credit for its 7 points.

If a team fails to reach their bid, then that team scores nothing, and the opposing team receives credit for the original bid they defeated,x plus the actual points they won during the hand.

For example: If your team wins the bid at the beginning of the game with a bid of 37 but took only 35 points in the hand, your team would score 0, and the opponents would score 44 points (their 7 points plus your bid of 37 points).

After each hand, the player to shuffle the tiles rotates to the left (clockwise). Play continues in this same manner.

The first team to reach 250 points wins. If both teams reach 250 points on the same hand, the team that made the bid on that final hand is the winner of the game, regardless of the score.

Variation: A simplified scoring system can be used with one "mark," or point, awarded for the victory of a hand. The first team to win 7 marks wins the match.

The instructions given here are probably sufficient for the beginner, but only serve as the basics of the game of Forty-Two. To learn more about the strategy of the game and for a more in-depth description of how the game is played, I suggest you refer to *Winning 42: Strategy & Lore of the National Game of Texas,*" by Dennis Roberson and published by Texas Tech Univer- sity Press in Lubbock, Texas, in 1997. The book also includes inter- esting information about the histo- ry of the game that I found to be very enjoyable reading.

SET VARIATIONS

Each of the following four games is a variation of the game of Forty-Two and each is played with two sets of double-6 dominoes. As a general rule, Eighty-Eight is the only game of the four that requires leading with a trump. When the game rules call for a player to lead with a trump, the game becomes more challenging.

Use this rule when playing the following games any time there are tiles in the boneyard after a hand is drawn: The highest bidder looks at the tiles in the boneyard. If one or both of the dominoes are count dominoes, the bidder must take the one or two count dominoes into his hand and remove the same number of tiles from his hand. Therefore, there will still be two tiles in the boneyard but neither will be a count domi- no. He should make this exchange of tiles without showing the tiles to any other player at the table.

Use the rules to Forty-Two, with the following variations.

Seventy-Nine

Domino set: Two sets of double-6 dominoes.

Number of players: 6, playing as two teams of 3 players per team.

Number of dominoes drawn: Each player draws 9 tiles. This leaves 2 tiles remaining in the boneyard.

The minimum bid is 50.

There are 9 tricks and each trick is worth one point.

Total of 79 points to be won in each hand: 70 (35 points in a dou- ble-6 set × 2 sets) + 9 (9 tricks at 1 point each) = 79.

Eighty

Domino set: Two sets of double-6 dominoes; remove all blank tiles.

Number of players: 4 players play as two teams of 2 players per team.

Number of dominoes drawn: Each player draws 10 tiles. This leaves 2 tiles remaining in the boneyard.

The minimum bid is 60.

There are 10 tricks and each trick is worth 2 points.

Total of 80 points to be won in each hand: 60 (30 points in a dou- ble-6 set with 7 blanks removed from the set × 2) + 20 (10 tricks at 2 points each) = 80.

Eighty-Four

Domino set: Two sets of double-6.
Number of players: 8 players play as two teams of 4 players per team or 6 players play as two teams of 3 players per team.
Number of dominoes drawn: When 8 play, each player draws 7 tiles and there are no tiles remaining in the boneyard. When 6 play, each player draws 9 tiles with 2 tiles remaining in the boneyard.

The minimum bid is 60.

With 8 players, there are 7 tricks and each trick is worth 2 points. With 6 players, there are 9 tricks and each trick is worth 2 points.

Total of 84 points to be won in each hand:
With 8 players: 70 (35 points in a double-6 set × 2) + 14 (7 tricks at 2 points each) = 84.

With 6 players: 70 (35 points in a double-6 set × 2) + 0 (tricks are worth nothing when playing this game with 6 players) + 14 (each double is worth one point when playing this game with 6 players) = 84.

Eighty-Eight

Domino set: Two sets of double-6.
Number of players: 6 players play as two teams with 3 players per team.
Number of dominoes drawn: Each player draws 9 tiles. This leaves 2 tiles remaining in the boneyard.

The minimum bid is 60.

There are 9 tricks and each trick is worth 2 points.

Total of 88 points to be won in each hand: 70 (35 points in a double-6 set × 2 sets) + 18 (9 tricks at 2 points each) = 88.

BIDDING VARIATIONS

The following bidding variations to the game of Forty-Two rely on the luck of the draw and make it possible for players to score more points with less skill and strategy.

Nel-O

The object of a Nel-O bid is to take no tricks. A Nel-O bidder's hand contains tiles so low he believes his opponents will be unable to force him to take a trick. If Nel-O is the winning bid, players must follow suit of the tile that is led on each trick, and there are no trumps.

When a player bids Nel-O, his partner must turn the tiles in his hand facedown on the table until the end of the hand, while the bidder plays out the hand with the opposing team. The bidder leads with the first tile. The opponents follow suit of the higher number of that tile. The player who wins the trick is in the lead. For the remainder of the hand, the goal of the opponents is to play lower tiles than the bidder. The bidder is set if he takes one trick.

Some Nel-O players treat doubles as a separate suit, with every player following suit with a double if a double is led. Most, however, do not play by this rule.

Plunge

The tactic of bidding Plunge allows for communication between partners during bidding and start of play about the tiles they hold in their hand. Once play begins, however, the hand plays out just like any regular Forty-Two hand.

If Plunge is the winning bid, the bidder's hand must contain at least four doubles and, by bidding Plunge, the bidder relays to his partner that he holds a great hand. The bid is automatically 168, and the bidder cannot lose a single trick. The bidder's partner is required to declare trumps, based on his own hand, and to lead by playing the first tile of the first trick.

When a player bids Plunge, he is gambling that he holds the double in his hand to the trumps and offs that his partner has yet to declare. The bidder takes a huge risk by bidding Plunge. If he is lucky, he and his partner match each other on most of the doubles and offs suits; if not, the consequence of his bid is a huge loss.

Sevens

Sevens is a bidding option that has no trumps or suits. The only thing that matters is the total sum of pips on the face of each tile in a bidder's hand. A player bidding Sevens believes he has more tiles in his hand whose pips total 7, or close to

7 (6 or 8), than any other player.

The bidder must bid at least 42 and cannot lose a single trick. The bidder plays his first tile, adding up to 7. Every other player must play a tile from his hand whose pips total 7 or the next-closest sum to 7. On each trick, every player must play the tile left in his hand whose pips total 7 or the tile whose pips total the closest to 7. A player does not have the option of saving that tile for play later in the hand. Play continues in this way. As tricks are played, they should remain in the middle of the table.

To set the bidder, at any point during a hand one of the opponents must play a tile whose total pips are closer to seven than the bidder's. A tie does not set the bidder.

Moon

In this game, bidding starts at 4 tricks and goes as high as 7, called "shooting the moon." There are only 3 players, and each bids or passes once. They can bid 7 or 21: 21 being the game. Failing costs the bidder the points/tricks he or she bid. The opponents get points for the tricks they captured. Tricks are 1 point.

All tiles with blanks, excepting only the double-blank, are removed from a double-6 set, leaving 22 tiles. Players each draw 7 tiles. The extra is the "widow" for the bidder's hand. If the tile is used, the bidder discards another tile.

Moon plays like 42, but with no "count" or partners. Pips are used as suits, with the double being highest.

Games for One Player

In each of the following games, shuffle the tiles, facedown, before drawing your hand.

It is important to be consistent in the manner in which you flip each tile over, from facedown to faceup. Choose which way you will turn tiles over and use that method throughout the game.

Fair Lucy

Domino set: Double-6.
Object of the game: To discard all the tiles in the set, two at a time, in pairs whose pips total 12.

Keeping the tiles facedown, draw 7 from the deck and place them facedown in a horizontal row in front of you. Draw 7 more tiles and, still keeping all tiles facedown, place one tile on top of each of the other 7 tiles. Draw 7 more tiles, and do the same. You should now have 7 stacks of tiles, each 3 tiles high. Then, take the remaining 7 undrawn tiles and place them faceup, one on top of each of the 7 stacks.

If any two faceup tiles have pips that together total 12, discard that pair of tiles. Then turn the tiles underneath the tiles that were just discarded to a faceup position.

Continue this process of discarding pairs of tiles whose sum totals exactly 12.

If you play the bottom tile of the stack, leaving fewer than 7 stacks of tiles, you may not move a tile to this "empty" spot to create a new stack.

At no time during the game should you have more than 7 tiles faceup.

Luzon

Domino set: Double-6.
Object of the game: To discard all the tiles in the set, two at a time, in pairs whose pips total 12.

Keeping the tiles facedown, place them in 5 vertical rows of 5 tiles each. Set aside the 3 remaining tiles.

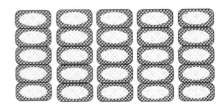

Turn each tile faceup, keeping them in their same positions. If the sum of the pips on any two tiles on the *bottom* horizontal row totals 12, discard that pair of tiles. The two lower tiles of the same vertical row may not be discarded at one time, even if their pips total 12.

The 3 tiles that were set aside at the beginning of the game may be used at any time during the game, as the player so chooses, to be coupled with any tile from the bottom of a vertical row.

In the course of the game you may end up with less than 5 vertical rows. If this occurs, it is permissible to move a tile from the bottom of any other vertical row in order to form another vertical row. At no point in the game, however, should there be more than 5 vertical rows. This rule is very important because if the 6-5 and the 0-1 or the 6-6 and the 0-0 were in the same vertical row it would be impossible to win without being able to move one of the two tiles to another vertical row.

This is a game of luck and skill. When you make a careful study of your exposed tiles, you will learn that some moves are much better than others.

Polka Dots

(aka Twelves)

Domino set: Double-6.

Object of the game: To discard all the tiles in the set two at a time, in pairs, when pips total 12.

Draw 6 tiles from the deck and place them faceup in a horizontal row in front of you.

If any two tiles in your tableau together have pips totaling exactly 12, remove those two tiles from your row and set them aside. Then, replace them by drawing two more tiles from the shuffled deck. Continue to do this, and win the game by discarding every tile in the deck.

If the situation arises that there is more than one pair of tiles whose pips total exactly 12, you may discard each and every pair of tiles before replacing your tableau with more tiles from the deck.

If a tile's pips can be added to more than one other tile in the tableau to get a total of 12 pips (for example: a 3-3 can be added to the 6-0 to total 12, or the 3-3 can be added to the 2-4 to total 12), you may discard any pair you choose.

Variations: 1) Use a tableau of 5 tiles for a more difficult game or a tableau of 4 tiles for an even more difficult game. You may also increase the number of tiles in your tableau to 7 for an easier game. 2) With adjustments, this game can be played with a set of dominoes other than the double-6 set. When playing with a double-9 set, the pips on two tiles in the tableau must total 18 in order to be discarded. The game may be played

VARIATION FOR FAIR LUCY, LUZON, AND POLKA DOTS

In the regular game, the 0-0 and the 6-6, and the 1-0 and the 6-5, must be matched to make 12, because there is no other way to match them. For the other tiles there are at least two ways each tile can be matched. Therefore, the 1-6 can be matched with the 4-1, 2-3, or 0-5. The game becomes much more difficult if you limit more of the tiles to only one possible match each. Try this variation: Require that each of the ends of the matching pair must total six.

The four remaining tiles (0-6, 1-5, 2-4, and 3-3) are tiles with 6 pips each and cannot be matched to another tile in the set so that the ends of the matching pair of tiles would total six. Therefore, the requirement that the ends of the matching pair of tiles total six will not apply to these four tiles; each of these four tiles may be matched with any one of the other three tiles to make a total of 12 pips for the pair, as in the original game.

in this way with any set of dominoes. Just take the total number of pips on the highest tile in the set (for example: 6 for a set of double-3 dominoes; 24 for a set of double-12 dominoes) and that is the number that two tiles in your tableau must total in order to be discarded.

Baronet

Domino set: May be played with any set of dominoes.
Object of the game: To remove all the dominoes from the line.

Keeping the tiles facedown, line them all up, side by side, in front of you.

Playing from left to right, with the first domino in the line considered the starting point, turn the dominoes faceup, one at a time, while counting "zero, one, two, three...." as each domino is turned faceup.

If the number spoken matches the total sum of the pips on that domino, remove that domino from the line. Continue counting where you left off, as you turn the next domino in line.

Counting begins with zero and ends with the number of pips on the highest double of the set of dominoes you are using for play (double-6: 12; double-7: 14; double-3: 6; double-9: 18; double-12: 24). If playing with a double-6 set of dominoes, count to 12, then begin counting with the number "zero" while turning the next domino in the line.

When you reach the end of the line, return to the first domino, continuing the count from the end of the line. If the number called on the last domino in line was "one," then "two" should be the number called while turning the first domino in line.

Keep repeating this process until all the dominoes in the line have been removed or until you cannot remove any more dominoes.

The Big Clock

(© 1996 by David Galt)

Domino set: Double-12.
Object of the game: To arrange the 12 double tiles from the set into a circular formation, each double being positioned in the same place as it would appear on a clock face. For example, the 1-1 tile would be placed in the formation in the same location the 1 would appear on a clock face; the 2-2 would be placed where the 2 would appear; and so on.

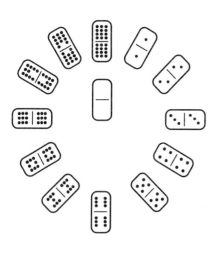

Remove the double-blank tile from the deck. Shuffle the remaining tiles, facedown. Draw 12 tiles,

and then place them, faceup, in a circular shape, placing the first tile at the point that will be considered "12:00" (where 12 would appear on a clock face), and continue by placing the second tile at "1:00," and so on, proceeding clockwise. Finally, place the double-blank tile inside your circle, at the very top, so as to "point to 12:00."

After the initial layout is finished, draw tiles one at a time from the deck, seeking to place each tile face up on top of another tile in your clock formation. When placing one tile on top of another, at least one end of the tile you are playing should match at least one end of the tile you are covering.

If you drew the 6-10, you could play it on the 3-10, 6-1, or 4-6. The best play, however, is likely to be on the 4-6 at the "10:00" time slot, in case you soon draw the 10-10.

By the way, never place a tile on top of a double, whether the double is in its correct time slot or not.

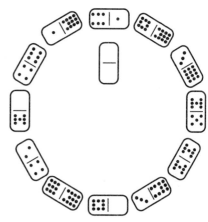

Except when it's a double tile, if you are unable to play the tile drawn from the deck because there is no match, place that tile aside, never to be drawn during the remainder of the game.

When you draw a double that has no match on the clock at all or when you have a double on the clock but in the wrong place, this is called a "double in trouble." The 7-7 at "4:00" in the drawing is a "double in trouble."

When you have a "double in trouble," you may move the top domino of any pile to the top of another pile, as long as at least one end of the tile being moved has the same number of pips as at least one end of the tile it is being placed on top of. Continue making as many such moves as necessary in order to bring any "double in trouble" to its correct time slot. You may even empty an entire time slot in this way, creating a blank space.

If you cannot fill a blank time slot with its correct double, fill it immediately with a new tile.

As soon as you place a double in its correct time slot, turn that tile, along with all the tiles underneath it, so it radiates out.

If you draw a double that cannot be played anywhere, the game is lost.

Variations: This game may be played with a double-9 set, in which case your clock face will not be a complete circle, starting with "1:00" and going only to "9:00."

You may also play this game with a set of double-6 dominoes, using a half-circle for your clock face or dealing the 6 tiles in a straight row, if you prefer.

The Buccaneer

Domino set: Double-6.
Object of the game: To get one of the seven doubles at the bottom of each stack and to have the remaining three dominoes in that stack be of the same suit as the double domino on the bottom of the stack.

Keeping the tiles facedown, place them in seven separate stacks of four dominoes each. Turn faceup the top domino on each of the seven stacks.

A domino may be moved from one stack to another if the number of pips on one end of the domino being moved matches the number of pips on one end of the domino onto which the move is made.

As the facedown dominoes are uncovered, turn them faceup and leave them on their stack. Never have more than five dominoes in any stack at any time.

If you play the bottom domino of any stack, leaving an "empty space," only a double domino may be used to start a new stack in that space.

Never turn a domino faceup unless it is the only domino in a stack or the top domino of the stack.

Castle Rock

Domino set: May be played with any set of dominoes.

Object of the game: To discard all the dominoes in the set.

Draw 3 tiles from the boneyard and turn them faceup, in a row. For explanatory purposes, let's call these three dominoes, from left to right, "Domino 1," "Domino 2," and "Domino 3."

If the pips on one end of Domino 1 match the pips on one end of Domino 3, then Domino 2 is removed from the row.

Continue to draw dominoes, always adding them to the right side, or end, of the row. When a match occurs between the ends of any two dominoes being separated by one domino, the domino in the middle of the matching dominoes is removed from the row.

Also, when a match occurs between the ends of three dominoes in a row, the player has the option of removing all three dominoes from the row. He or she may decide it is not the best strategy to remove all three dominoes, depending on what the situation will be like after either move. However, the player must always remove at least one domino when the opportunity arises.

Should you discard all the dominoes from the array, you simply draw from the stock to start a new array as at the beginning. Keep repeating this process until you have discarded all dominoes in the set or until you cannot discard any more dominoes.

Five-Up Solitaire

Domino set: Double-6. Draw 5 tiles from the deck. Set any tile, and then play as many tiles from your hand as possible. Continue to play using the same rules you would use with 2 or more players.

When playing this game, you may wish to play against the deck, keeping separate scores: one for you and one for the deck. Try these ideas: At the beginning of each hand, give the deck 5 points if you're a beginner and 10 points if you're more experienced. This will offset the scores you will make during play. The deck receives 3 points if you overdraw. If the game ends in block, the deck receives the points left in your hand. If your total score is 61 points or more and you are ahead at the end of that hand, you have won the game. If the deck has a total score of 61 points or more and is ahead at the end of that hand, the deck wins the game.

Good Neighbors

(© 1996 by David Galt)

Domino set: Double-12.

Object of the game: To pair up and remove all the dominoes but one.

Keeping the tiles in a facedown position, draw 12 from the deck and place them in three horizontal rows of 4 tiles per row. Now, turn them faceup in place. This is your tableau.

You may remove from your tableau pairs of tiles that are "good neighbors" "Good neighbors" are tiles that are next to each other (including diagonally) and have matching ends. (At least one end of one tile has to have the same number of pips as at least one end of the other tile.)

On each turn, remove at least one pair of "good neighbors." (You may remove more than one pair if you like.) In this layout, there are several "good neighbor" pairs to choose from: 6-1 + 12-6; 9-12 + 12-6; 9-12 + 12-3; 3-2 + 3-1; 3-2 + 5-3; and 9-3 + 3-1.

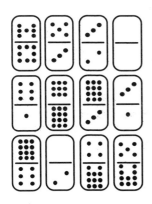

When a pair (or pairs) is removed from your tableau, this leaves empty spaces. All the remaining tiles should be moved towards the upper left-hand corner of your tableau. This is done

first by moving any remaining tiles having one or more empty spaces to their left, over to the left, filling in that space (those spaces). Then move tiles from the left-hand side of the middle row up to the right-hand side of the top row and tiles from the left-hand side of the bottom row up to the right-hand side of the middle row. After this is done, draw tiles from the deck and place them in the empty spaces of the tableau, left to right, and top to bottom, making your tableau once again, 3 horizontal rows of 4 tiles per row.

Example: Let's say you remove the 3-2 + 3-1 and 6-1 + 12-6 from your tableau. Move 0-0 over to the left; bring 9-12 up to the top row; move 12-3 to the left; bring the bottom three tiles up one row; pick 4 new tiles from the deck and place them, left to right, on the bottom row.

In this way, pair, remove, and fill-in repeatedly. You lose the game any time you are "stuck" and have no "good neighbors" to remove from your tableau.

Variations: This game may be played with a double-9 set, in which case your tableau should be 3 horizontal rows of 3 tiles per row. The object is to remove all dominoes but one when playing with a double-9 set.

Or you may play this game with a set of double-6 dominoes, with a tableau of two horizontal rows of 6 tiles per row. The object when playing with a double-6 set is to remove all dominoes.

The Jubilee

Domino set: Double-6.

Object of the game: To transfer all the tiles from the several stacks to a particular formation of tiles.

Keeping the tiles in a facedown position, draw 7 from the deck and place them in a horizontal row in front of you with sides touching.

Draw 6 more tiles and, still keeping all the tiles facedown, place one tile on top of each of the other tiles, leaving the far left-hand tile uncovered. Now draw 5 tiles, and add these to the top of each of the other tiles, leaving the two far left-hand tiles uncovered. Now draw 4 tiles, then 3, and so on, continuing to place your tiles, facedown, on top of your horizontal row from right to left.

When done, you should have 7 stacks of tiles, facedown, sides touching, containing the following number of tiles in each stack, from left to right: 1, 2, 3, 4, 5, 6, 7. Turn the tile on top of each stack, 7 in all, faceup.

Only tiles from the top of each stack may be moved. They may be moved from one stack to another stack or from a stack to the formation shown at above right. It is permissible for a stack to contain more than 7 tiles during the course of the game; however, there should never be more than 7 stacks at a time.

Any time you have a facedown tile at the top of a stack (this will happen after you have moved a faceup tile in order to make a play), you should turn this tile faceup.

When every tile in a stack is played, leaving an "empty" spot, a new stack may be started in that place—but only with a double, and that double must come from the top of another stack.

It is against the rules to look at any of the tiles that are not already turned faceup at the top of each stack, however.

Patience

(aka Little Harp)

Domino set: Double-6.

Object of the game: To have all tiles turned faceup in 7 or less vertical rows.

Keeping the tiles facedown, place them in 7 rows. The first row contains 7 tiles; the second row contains 6; and so on, each row containing one less tile and the last row containing only one tile. Then, turn the far left tile of each horizontal row faceup.

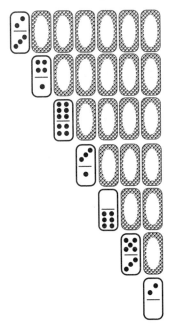

Choose the way you will turn tiles over from facedown to faceup and use that method consistently throughout the game.

Move the faceup tiles from one row to another, placing matching end to matching end, without turning the tile around.

Any time you have a facedown tile at the end of a row (this happens after you have moved a faceup tile in order to make a play), you should turn this tile faceup.

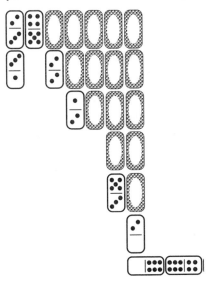

In the course of the game you may end up with less than 7 vertical rows. If this occurs, it is permissible to move a tile or a full or partial horizontal row of matching tiles, in order to form another vertical row. At no point in the game, however, should there be more than 7 vertical rows.

Squeeze

(© 1996 by David Galt)

Domino set: Double-12, double-9, or double-6.

Object of the game: To have no dominoes left at the end of the game.

To have one or two dominoes left at the end of the game is considered a very near win.

Keeping the tiles facedown, draw 7 tiles from the deck and place them in a horizontal row in front of you.

You may remove any pair of tiles that have matching ends (at least one end of one tile has to have the same number of pips as at least one end of the other tile) and which are separated by one or two tiles in the tableau. In addition, you may remove any 3 or more tiles in a row that have matching ends. If there is more than one possible play, you may choose which move to make.

After removing tiles from your tableau in this way, just squeeze the remaining tiles in the row closer together. Then remove more tiles from your tableau, if possible, until all possible plays have been made. Once it is not possible to remove any more tiles, draw 7 new tiles from the deck and add them to the end (right side) of the row.

Continue this process of matching, removing, then adding more tiles to your row until you have won the game by removing all tiles from your tableau or until the game is lost because you are unable to remove the remaining tiles in your tableau.

Note: It takes both planning and luck to finish with no tiles left. For your final play, you'll need to have 3 or more tiles in a row with matching ends.

Stack

Domino set: Double-6.

Object of the game: To play all dominoes in the deck by matching them, one at a time, to one of the eight exposed ends in the tableau.

Draw 4 tiles from the deck and place them faceup in a horizontal row in front of you.

Next, draw another tile from the deck. Make a play by matching one end of that tile to one of the eight exposed ends in your tableau. Continue in this manner by drawing tiles, one at a time, from the deck and then matching one end of the tiles to an open end in your tableau.

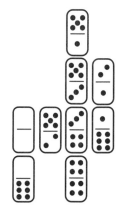

If at any time there is no match and a play cannot be made, the game is over and you have lost. If you succeed in playing all 28 dominoes, by matching them with another tile in your tableau, you have won the game.

Variations: For a more challenging game, start the game by drawing 3 tiles instead of 4. For a less difficult game, draw 5—or even 6—tiles at the start of the game.

The Sultan

Domino set: Double-6.
Object of the game: To discard all the tiles in the row, two at a time, in pairs whose ends, sides touching, match horizontally.

Keeping the tiles in a facedown position, place all the tiles in the deck in a horizontal row in front of you with sides touching. Then turn the tiles over to a faceup position and do not remove them from their original order in the row. Choose which way you will turn tiles over, from facedown to faceup, and use that method consistently throughout the game.

From your row of 28, discard any two tiles that have adjoining ends that match horizontally. Do not discard adjoining tiles with ends that match only vertically.

After discarding a pair of tiles from your row, move the tiles in your row closer together to take up the space in the row and so that all sides of each tile in the row are touching.

This is a game of luck and skill. When you make a careful study of your exposed tiles, you will learn that some moves are much better than others.

Sympathy

Domino set: Double-6.
Object of the game: To discard all but one tile in the set by removing each tile one at a time and leaving only the 6-6 remaining in your tableau at the end of the game.

Draw 4 tiles from the deck and place them faceup in a horizontal row in front of you.

Remove any tile in the tableau that has exactly one pip less than any other tile in the tableau.

Draw 4 more tiles and place them, faceup, on top of the three remaining tiles in your tableau and in the "empty" space of the tile removed with the first play. The tiles underneath other tiles should be completely covered so that none of the pips are showing.

Again, remove any tile in the tableau that has exactly one pip less than any other tile in the tableau, as you did with your first play. Then draw 4 more tiles, and so on, continuing in this same manner throughout the game. If at any point in the game there is more than one play that could be made, it is usually best to remove the tile with the lowest number of pips.

Traffic

(© 1994 by David Galt)

Domino set: Double-12, double-9, or double-6.

Object of the game: To use up all the tiles by playing them in quads. A *quad* is four consecutive numbers running in ascending or descending order, and played in a straight line. Blanks count only as 0 in 0-1-2-3.

When playing with a double-6 set, draw 4 tiles; a double-9 set, draw 5; and, a double-12 set, draw 6. Return to this same number of tiles after each turn.

Draw the correct number of tiles from the deck, then place them, faceup, in front of you. Use 2, 3, or 4 of the tiles drawn to make four numbers in a row: a quad. For example, playing with a set of double-6 dominoes, you draw 3-6, 1-2, 2-4, and 5-5. Begin play with a quad of all four tiles or with a quad of three tiles.

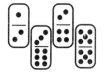 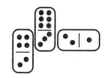

Once you have made a quad, leave it in your tableau and continue the process by again drawing the correct number of tiles from the deck.

Continue to draw more tiles from the deck one at a time, attaching enough new tiles to a number played already to make a new quad. But, if at any turn you can't make a quad, you lose. After awhile, your dominoes will start forming a real traffic snarl!"

To make a new quad, you will usually add 2 or 3 dominoes. Sometimes you can do it with just one. This must be a domino with consecutive numbers that you can attach in sequence. For instance, you can play 7-6 after 9-8 — or before 5-4—if either is available.

As long as you make a quad at each turn, other number sequences you make don't matter at all.

Just be sure to observe these don'ts:

- Don't move any dominoes already played.
- Don't make a straight line of five or more numbers in a row. Four is the limit!

Games Using Special Domino Sets

The games in this section are played with special sets of dominoes. Four of the games—Doublecross, Pip, Spinner, and Wildstar—are played with a set of dominoes that includes 55 tiles (a double-9 set of dominoes) plus wild tiles and/or directional tiles that come with the game.

The game of Spoiler is played with a special 48-tile set, with "link" and "dead end" tiles, and a hexagon starter piece. A center starter piece is also included with the games of Pip and Wildstar.

The RaceHorse game uses a special 28-tile set of dominoes with numerals instead of pips.

Doublecross

(© 1990 by Gamesource)

Domino set: 48 playing tiles; one score pad.

Object of the game: To be the first player or team to accumulate 500 points.

Number of tiles drawn: If 2 or 3 play, each draws 12 tiles; 4 or 5 play, each draws 9; and if 6 play, each draws 8 tiles. (If 6 play, there will be no remaining tiles after the draw, therefore, there will be no drawing during the game.)

Place all the tiles facedown and shuffle.

The player with the triple-6 tile begins the round by placing the tile faceup on the playing surface. If the triple-6 is not drawn, the next-highest triple starts the round.

The play proceeds in a clockwise manner.

If a player is unable to place a tile from his hand, he draws one tile from the draw pile.

If a player is still unable to place a tile, play passes to the next player.

Each round ends when any player plays all the tiles in his hand. All other players add up their remaining tiles, and those points are awarded to the winner of the round.

In team play, only the opposing team's points are added to the winning team's score.

Scoring:

QUAD SCORE: Player matches one or

two sections of a tile to form a quad. Point value: 12 points.

DOUBLE QUAD SCORE: Player matches two sections to form two quads. Point value: 22 points.

BRIDGE SCORE: A tile is used to connect the ends of two existing tiles. Point value: 6 points.

T-BRIDGE SCORE: A tile is placed using the middle section and only one end to match an existing pattern. Point value: 20 points.

DOUBLE SCORE: Player matches a tile that forms one quad and two additional sections. Point value: 30 points.

TRIPLE SCORE: Occurs only when a tile is placed parallel to an existing pattern and all 3 sections match. Point value: 28 points.

DOUBLECROSS: Player places a triple tile to match an existing pattern. The point value of a doublecross is the sum × 2. Point value: 24 × 2 = 48 points!

Note: The first score occurs when the first quad is formed.

Pip

(© 1991 by Michael Poor)

Domino set: The game is played with a special set of dominoes that includes a double-9 set (55 pieces), plus 11 wild "pip" tiles, 4 directional tiles (S, R, A, D) with wild "pip" ends, for a total of 70 tiles, and 1 game-starter center piece.

Directional tiles may be used at any time to create strategic plays. They are:

"S" (**skip tile**): Play skips the next player.

"R" (reverse tile): Reverses the direction of play.

"A" (play-again tile): Allows that player an additional turn.

"D" (draw tile): Forces the next player to draw an additional tile from those remaining in the stock pile. If no stock pile is available, the player using the draw tile passes a tile from his hand to the next player.

Each directional tile also has a wild pip design at its opposite end which is wild and may be played as any number.

Wild-pip tiles: There are 11 wild-pip tiles, which may be played as any number. The wild double-pip tile must be played as a double number only.

Number of players: 2 or more.

Object of the game: To be the player with the lowest score after nine rounds of play.

Choose one player to be the scorekeeper. Keeping the tiles face-down on the table, each player draws 9 tiles from the deck. The remaining tiles comprise the stock pile. With 2 players only, each draws 15 tiles.

The player with the 1-1 tile (or the double "pip" tile in the event

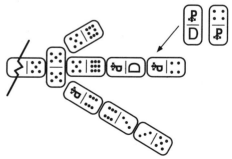

the 1-1 is not drawn) begins the round by placing it faceup in the center slot of the wooden center piece. If the double-pip tile is used to begin any round, it will represent the number tile for that round. (For example: Round 4 begins with the 4-4 tile or the double-pip tile. If the double-pip tile is used to begin that round, it represents the 4-4 tile.) Each round begins with the double tile next in value (e.g., double-2, 3, 4, 5, progressing through 9). There are nine rounds in a game.

If neither the 1-1 nor the double-pip tile is drawn, the designated scorekeeper draws one tile from the stock pile. Each player continues to draw from the stock pile in a clockwise manner until the 1-1 or the double-pip tile is drawn.

Play proceeds in a clockwise manner.

The second player may play on either side of the starting tile, using a 1 or a wild-pip tile, placing it horizontally against the first tile played.

The third and all subsequent players may place their tile on either the unplayed side of the original domino or on the previously played domino. Players are free to play on either side of any domino (or on the top and bottom of the 1-1 or pip tile) only when both sides of the starting tile have had play.

A player using a double tile places it vertically on the playing surface.

When a double tile is played

(except for the initial start-of-the-game play), the next three plays must be played on the double using either a corresponding-number tile or a wild-pip tile. Play may then proceed from any "branch" on the playing surface.

If a player is unable to place a tile from his hand, he draws one tile from the stock pile. If he is still unable to place a domino, play passes to the next person.

The round is over when a player has played all the tiles in his hand or when a round is blocked. A round is blocked when no player can place a tile from his hand, and the stock pile has been depleted.

When the round is over because a player has played all the tiles in his hand, that player is considered the winner for that round. In the case of the round ending in a block, all tiles remaining in each player's hand are counted and added to their scores. There is no winner for that round, and no player may deduct any points from his score.

Scoring: At the end of every round, each player totals the count of each tile remaining in his hand. Count is determined by the total number of pips of each tile, in addition to the points from any wild tiles as follows:

Single wild-pip tiles count 20 points each, plus the number of dots on the tile.

Double wild-pip tiles count 50 points each.

Each directional tile counts as

25 points, not including the "pips" on the tile which are an additional 20 points. The points are totaled, and the scorekeeper records each player's total. The scorekeeper then deducts 10 points from the round winner's score.

Note: No player's score may fall below zero.

RaceHorse

(© 1990 by Ferman C. Rice)

The creator of this game, Ferman Rice, said, "The reason the game is called RaceHorse is because you can come back from the stretch to the lead in a short period of time. It's a game that when you are down, you don't have to despair."

Domino set: The game is played with a special 28-tile set of dominoes bearing numerals instead of pips. These tiles are called "horses."

Number of players: 2 to 4 players.

Object of the game: To be the first player to earn a score of 250.

Shuffle the tiles face (numbered side) down. Then, each player draws one tile from the deck. The player who turns over the horse with the highest number gets to play first. After this, play rotates back and forth or around the table.

+12

| 9 | 6 |

| 6 |

| 3 |

+3

After reshuffling the tiles, each player draws his hand from the deck.

Number of dominoes drawn: For 2 players, 7 horses each; for 3 players, 6 horses each; for 4 players, 5 horses each. The remaining horses are set aside to be drawn as needed.

This game is basically the game of Five-Up, with some additions.

Set: Any domino may be used as set.

Each player tries to match the number on one end of a tile from his hand with the number on an open end of any tile in the layout. Color coding simplifies this.

A player is awarded points every time he makes a play that results in the open ends of the tiles in the line of play adding up to a multiple of 5. (5 points for 5 pips; 10 points for 10 pips; 15 points for 15 pips; and so on.) Each player must announce his points on making his play in order to receive credit for the points made.

The player who dominoes is also awarded points at the end of each hand by adding up, and rounding to the nearest multiple of 5, the pips on the tiles left in his opponents' hands.

When a player scores, he must play again until he can no longer score. At that point, he plays one more tile before it becomes the other player's turn. Scores must be counted after each play.

Horses with double numbers are called "daily doubles"; when played, they entitle the player to play again. Points on the ends of the daily doubles count only after they have been played on—unless they are a dead end.

A play cannot be made on the end of a daily double until after plays have been made on both sides—unless it dead ends.

When a player cannot play, he

must draw a horse. If he still cannot play, he must keep drawing until he can. If he scores, he must play again, or draw until he can play.

In the event a player can't play, and there are no more horses left to draw, he must pass his turn to the next player.

If a player plays a scoring tile or a daily double, he must draw until he can play again.

The first player to play his last horse gets to keep the points left in his opponent's hand and adds them to his score, rounding to the nearest 5 points.

If the first horse you play is a 5 or 10 tile, or may be added together with the open ends of the layout to total 5 or 10 points, you receive those points and play again.

Only the points on the ends of the horses count.

There are no "9" dominoes in the game. Be careful not to mistake the "6" tile for a "9."

Spinner™

(© 1997 by Gamesource, 1983 by Dr. James F. & Edna Graham)

Domino set: The game is played with a special set of dominoes that includes a full set of double-9 dominoes plus 11 extra "spinner" dominoes, for a total of 66 domino tiles.

Number of players: 2 to 8 players.

Object of the game: To be the player with the lowest score.

Number of dominoes drawn: If 2 players, draw 14 dominoes each. If 3 to 8 players, draw 7 dominoes each. The remaining domino tiles make up the boneyard.

Spinners are wild.

Set: The first domino played must be the 9-9 or a double-spinner as a substitute for the 9-9. If no player has a 9-9 or double-spinner, the player who shuffled the dominoes draws one domino from the boneyard. Play continues to the left, each player drawing one domino from the boneyard until a 9-9 or double-spinner is drawn and then set.

Once the 9-9 or double-spinner is drawn, it is placed in the center of the table. The second and third play must be a 9 or a wild spinner. Players must draw one domino from the reserve pile each time they do not have a domino to play from their hand.

After each double is played, the next 3 plays must be placed on that double. The tiles played on the double must have either a matching end to the double in the layout or a spinner. Each player who does not have a tile with a matching end or a spinner must draw 1 domino from the reserve pile. Unless a domino is drawn that will play, the player passes.

Upon completion of 3 dominoes played on the double, the following player is free to play on any end of the layout—either matching the end domino or playing a spinner. Play your large domino if possible; this will stop the next player from discarding a large double.

Continue play until one player wins the hand by playing all the dominoes in his or her hand. The pips plus spinners are counted on all unplayed dominoes left in each player's hand at the end of each hand. Each player gives the total number to the scorekeeper.

Continue the game by starting the next hand with the 8-8 tile or the double-spinner; the following hand with the 7-7 or the double-spinner; and so on, the last hand beginning with the 0-0 as set domino.

The winner of the previous hand always shuffles for the next hand and is the first player to draw from the boneyard if no player holds the correct double to set or a double-spinner.

At the end of each game, add each player's total score. The player with the lowest score is the winner.

Players may agree, prior to the start of any game, to play a shorter game. To shorten the game, in the first round the player holding the 9-9 sets. If no one holds the 9-9, the player holding the 8-8 sets. If no one holds the 8-8, the player holding the 7-7 sets, and so on.

Spoiler
(© 1994 by David W. Crump)

David Crump had been in the toy, hobby, and game business for a good many years as a retailer before creating Spoiler. He has also designed credits for several military simulation games. Spoiler was created while driving between his game stores in Dallas, Texas. First, the idea of the hexagon starter piece came to mind. Next, while approaching the tollbooth of the North Dallas Tollway, the "dead end" piece was envisioned. The game also incorporates the "link," or wild card, common in many games. The special doubles play evolved in play testing. Credit for the game's title goes to David's wife, Rosanne. It was her idea to call the piece with both a "link" and a "dead end" a "spoiler" because it spoils an opponent's upcoming play.

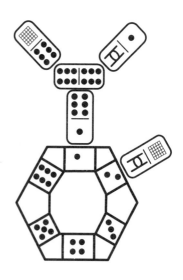

Domino set: A special 48-tile set, with "link" and "dead end" tiles, and a hexagon starter piece.

Object of the game: To be the first to earn a score of at least 100 points times the number of players. (For example: If there are 4 players, the winning score is 400 points or more.)

Spoiler is played in rounds. In each round, you try to get rid of all your tiles first. Branch your "doubles" and play an extra domino on each of the doubles in your same turn. Block your opponents' moves with the special "dead end." Use your dominoes with link ends when you are stuck. The quicker you are out of tiles, the more dominoes everyone else will have left in their hand and the larger your score will be.

Mix all the dominoes facedown. The first player is determined by drawing a single domino. The player who draws the highest value domino (see "Scoring" for values) plays first. The first player of each subsequent round rotates one player to the left (clockwise).

For games with 4 to 6 players, the dominoes are dealt out equally to each player. For games of 2 or 3 players, deal 12 tiles per player. In both cases, set aside any remaining tiles.

Play begins with the hexagon placed in the center of the table. The round's first player makes either a normal play or a special play (see "Special Plays") using any side of the hexagon. A normal play is made by placing a domino

end to end with a side of the hexagon or any domino that has a matching end. Play continues to the left with each player making a normal play, a special play, or passing. A player without any legal move must pass.

Special plays: A "link" is a domino end with an interlocked chain symbol. This special end will link with any domino end except the "dead end." A domino with only one "link" cannot be used as a "double."

A "double link" can be used as any double and new branches created (see "Doubles").

A "dead end" is a domino end with a brick wall symbol. A dead end will not connect to any other end and blocks further play on the branch. A deadend is played with the other end matched to the branch. There is no "double dead end."

The "spoiler" is a domino that has both a link and a dead end (a link on one end and a dead end on the other end). This special domino allows you to put a stop to play on any branch but is worth 20 points if you're caught with it in your hand at the end of a round.

Doubles: A "double" is a domino with identical ends. A double can be played like any domino by matching it end to end, but it can also be used for "branching," by matching it sideways to a matching end. A double used to branch is first played sideways and then the player has the option, during the same turn, of playing an additional domino on each end of the new branch. These additional dominoes are positioned at 45-degree angles to the double's ends and pointed away from the center hexagon. This is a very advantageous play, particularly if you can play all three dominoes.

A round ends when no player has a legal play, all players pass (whether they have a legal play or not), or when a player "goes out" by playing his last domino.

At the end of each round, a winner is determined and a score for the winner is calculated.

Scoring: If a player is the first player to play the last tile in his hand, he is automatically the winner and wins all the points of all remaining dominoes in his opponents' hands.

If the round ends because all players pass or have no legal plays, then the winner is the player with the lowest point value of dominoes remaining in his hand at the end of the round. In this case, the winner receives the points of all unplayed dominoes of the other players less points of his own unplayed dominoes.

In the unlikely event that more than one player has the same low score (a tie), then they are co-winners. The points of the unplayed dominoes of all other players are totaled and split (rounded up) between the co-winners. Next, they subtract their own points for their final score (minimum score of 1).

The point value of each domino is the number of dots on both ends.

The special dead end and link ends are valued at 10 points each.

Spoiler variations: For a shorter game, play to a winning score of 50 points per player. A normal game of Spoiler plays in about 2 hours, depending on the number of players. The shorter game plays in about an hour.

To play with more players (up to 8 players), combine two sets of Spoiler and play in this way: Each player is dealt 12 tiles with remaining tiles set aside. The winning score is 50 points times the number of players. (For example: If 7 are playing, the winning score is 350 points or more.) You will need a large table.

Wildstar

(© 1995 by Plastech Industries)

Domino set: Game is played with a special set of dominoes that includes a double-9 set (55 pieces) plus 5 extra dominoes, "wildstars," for a total of 60 dominoes and a center starter piece.

Object of the game: To be the first player to dispose of all your dominoes.

Number of players: 2 to 8 players.

First, shuffle the dominoes, facedown, at the beginning of the game. Then each player draws his hand.

Number of dominoes drawn: If 2 players, draw 20 dominoes each. If 3 to 5 players, draw 10 dominoes each. If 6 to 8 players, draw 7 dominoes each. The remaining dominoes make up the boneyard.

After drawing the needed dominoes at the beginning of each hand, the remaining tiles are set aside to be drawn as needed by the players. This is called the "draw pile." For players' convenience, there may be more than one "draw pile" on the table with each player free to draw from any pile.

All wildstar dominoes are wild and can be substituted for any domino—blank through 9—in horizontal or vertical direction, with these two exceptions:

• The double star (wildstar) may not be used as a center domino.
• The five dominoes played around the center must be matching-numbered dominoes—no wildstar. Star dominoes then may be used on all later plays.

The count: Each dot on a domino counts 1 point. (Example: The 6-5 counts 11 points.)

Each wildstar counts 20 points. 0-0 counts 30 points.

The first play of the first round begins with the 9-9 tile. The player holding the 9-9 places that tile in the star center piece to begin the game. Each hand thereafter begins with the next-lowest number double tile. (For example: The first hand begins with the 9-9; the second with the 8-8; and so on, continuing down through the 0-0.)

If no player holds the correct double to begin that round, then the person who shuffled the dominoes draws a domino from the "pile." If the shuffler does not draw the correct double, then the drawing continues around the table until one is drawn.

Once the first play of that round has been made, play continues clockwise around the table. The next five plays must be made with tiles that have an end with the same number as the center tile. If a player cannot make a play on the center tile, he must draw a tile from the pile. If the player draws a playable tile, then he may play it. If not, that tile is added to the player's hand and play moves on to the next person.

Once five matching dominoes have been played on the center tile, a player may play any domino from his hand whose end matches the open end of a domino played on the table. A player also has the option of playing a double domino or wildstar domino.

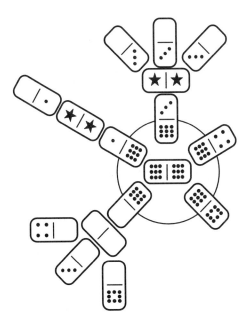

The first player to play all his or her dominoes is the winner of the hand. The other players determine the count of the dominoes remaining in their hands and give their score to the winner of that hand. (See "Partners" if playing as teams.)

In the event the game becomes blocked (no player can make a play), everyone makes a count of their dominoes and that score is added to each person's score or each team's score.

The person winning the previous hand shuffles the tiles for the next hand, and is the first player of the next round.

At the end of the game, the person or team with the lowest score is the winner.

Partners: If an even number of people are playing, they may divide into two teams, sitting alternately around the table. When a member of one team plays the last domino in his hand, only the dominoes left remaining in the hands of the other team are counted and recorded.

Games Using Oriental Dominoes

All the games in this category are played with a set of Oriental Dominoes, sometimes called Chinese Dominoes. Oriental, or Chinese, domino sets differ from Western, or European, dominoes in several ways.

There are 32 tiles in a set of Oriental dominoes (as opposed to a European double-6 set of 28 tiles); there are no blank ends; 11 of the tiles are duplicated; and most Oriental dominoes are larger than their European counterparts. Oriental sets containing up to 141 tiles are known, but the extra tiles are duplicates of the basic 21. If you were to take a European double-6 set of dominoes and remove all the blank tiles, then duplicate 11 of the tiles (6-6; 6-5; 6-4; 6-1; 5-5; 5-1; 4-4; 3-3; 3-1; 2-2; and 1-1), you would have an Oriental set.

All Oriental dominoes—Chinese, Korean, Burmese, and Thai—consist of 21 pieces representing all the possible throws of a pair of 6-sided dice. Oriental dice have the ones and fours marked with red pips instead of black, and Oriental dominoes are marked in the same way. In addition, three of the pips at each end of the 6-6 tile are red, though the 6 pips of the corresponding dice are black. These red pips are important in some games. Also, the pip on the end of a tile from the one suit is larger than the pips on the other dominoes and dice.

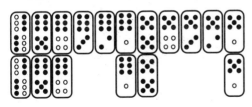

The names of the various pairs of domino tiles (for example: Supreme, Heaven, Earth, and Man) are the same as the names of the various combinations that can be tossed with a pair of dice.

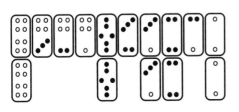

The 11 pairs of *duplicate* tiles (22 tiles) in the Oriental set seen at left make up what is called the "civil" series; the remaining 10 non-duplicate tiles in the set form what is called the "military" series.

Bullfighting

(Tau ngau)

Additional equipment: 1 pair of dice to be thrown at the start of the round to determine the "banker."
Object of the game: To beat the bull.
Number of players: 3 to 6 players.

Any number of onlookers may place stakes alongside those of a player of their choice.

Dice are thrown to determine the banker.

The dominoes are shuffled, facedown. Keeping the tiles facedown, each player, including the banker, draws five dominoes. Before looking at their tiles, the players place their stakes in front of them to any limit which may be imposed by the banker. When the stakes have been placed, the players look at their tiles. The value of each tile depends upon its number of pips, except that the 2-1 and 4-2 tiles each may count as 3 points or 6 points.

Every player must discard 3 tiles from his hand which, when added together, total 10, 20, or 30 points. Examples:

    3-1 + 2-2 + 1-1 = 10
    6-6 + 3-3 + 1-1 = 20
        (a multiple of 10)
    2-1 + 6-5 + 3-3 = 20
        (the 2-1 counting as 3 points)
    2-1 + 4-4 + 3-3 = 20
        (the 2-1 counting as 6 points)

After discarding 3 tiles, the 2 remaining tiles in each player's hand are exposed. Each player counts the pips on the two exposed tiles and receives a score of 1 point per each pip. In the case

when their score is 10 points or more, the first digit of that number is removed. For example, 12 pips would count as 2.

If a player's score is less than the banker's, he loses his stake to the banker; if his score is more than the banker's, the banker pays him the equivalent of his stake. If a player and the banker have equal scores, there is no exchange between them.

If a player cannot discard 3 tiles to form 10 points, or a multiple of 10, he is "stuck," in which case the banker takes his stake. If the banker is "stuck," he pays the equivalent stake to all the players who are able to discard 3 tiles—and not to any players who are "stuck."

When a banker scores points, the player on his right becomes the new banker for the next round. If the banker is "stuck," he remains banker for another round.

After each round, all 32 tiles are shuffled together and then each player draws 5 tiles and the game continues as before.

Collecting Tens

(K'ap t'ai shap)

Popular in Chinese gambling houses in the U.S., this game and one called Playing Heavens and Nines (*Ta t'in kau*) were the forerunner of the tile game Mah-jongg, which swept the Western World in the 1920s.

Domino set: Many sets of Oriental dominoes are used.
Additional equipment: 4 dice and a cup.

Number of players: 2 or more.

Object of the game: To be the first player to collect 10 tiles consisting of a matching pair of two identical tiles, and four decimal pairs, the sum of the pips of each pair being 10 or a multiple of 10.

Tiles are carefully mixed by the players and piled facedown, 5 tiles high, in a long "woodpile" down the center of the table. At the start of the game, all players place equal wagers in a box on the table. The house takes 5% of the total; the rest goes to the winning player.

The croupier or one of the players shakes 4 dice under a cup, then throws them on the table. That player then counts each player, counterclockwise around the table, starting with the player on his right, and continues to count until he reaches the number thrown. Where the counting ends, that player becomes the leader.

The top tile on the third stack from the end of the pile is removed. The top tile from each alternate stack up to one less than the number of players is also removed. These tiles are placed at the far end of the pile.

The leader takes the 2 stacks at the end, containing 10 tiles. The second player on his right takes the next 2 stacks, containing 9 tiles. The remaining players each take 9 tiles.

The players examine their tiles. If the leader has not drawn a winning hand, he discards a tile and places it faceup on the table.

The next player on his right may pick up the tile the first player discarded to complete a winning hand, or he may exchange it for a tile from his hand, which he places faceup on the table. He also draws a tile from the top of the exposed stack of the woodpile. If it does not complete a winning hand, he may either place it faceup on the table or keep it and discard a tile from his hand.

The third player may then take one of the tiles from the table and draw one from the top of the exposed stack. The game continues until one of the players wins by collecting 10 tiles: a matching pair of two identical tiles and four decimal pairs, the sum of the pips of each pair being 10 or a multiple of 10. The tile 2-4 only counts as three when making up tens.

The winner of a game takes the contents of the stake box and a new game begins.

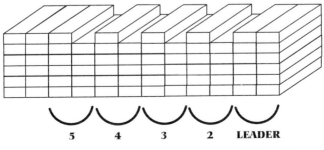

| 5 | 4 | 3 | 2 | LEADER |

Disputing Tens

(Tsung shap)

Object of the game: To be the player with the highest count at the end of the game.

Number of players: 2 players.

The tiles are placed facedown, side by side, in a "woodpile" 4 tiles high and 8 tiles long. The players divide the woodpile between them, each taking 4 stacks. The first player draws the top tile from the stack at the right of his pile and lays it faceup on the table. The second player then draws a tile from his pile and lays it faceup alongside the tile played by the first player. They continue to draw and place the tiles on the table at either end of the row of upturned tiles.

When a tile is played that matches one of the tiles at either end of the row, the player making that play removes both tiles from the row. At the end of the game, they count 10 points for each pip on them.

When a tile is played whose pips make a multiple of 10 when added to the pips on the tiles at both ends of the row, the player making that play removes the tiles from the row. At the end of the game, each pip on them counts 1 point.

When a tile is played whose pips make a multiple of 10 when added with the pips on the two tiles at either end of the row, the player making that play removes the three tiles from the row.

At the end of the game, each pip on them counts 1 point.

If there are only 2 tiles on the table and a player takes them, he piles them on top of each other to mark a "sweep." A sweep counts 40 points. He then draws from his pile and lays out another tile.

If a player fails to take up a winning combination of 2 or 3 tiles, his opponent may take it, then lay out a tile and continue the game.

The game ends when one of the players has played all his tiles.

Fishing

(Tiu u)

Domino set: 2 sets of Oriental dominoes (Each set contains 32 tiles; 2 sets = 64 tiles total.)

Object of the game: To be the player with the highest count at the end of the game.

Number of players: 2, 3, or 4.

Keeping the tiles facedown, place them in 16 stacks of 4 tiles per stack. This is called a "woodpile." If there are 4 players, each player removes 1 stack from one side of the woodpile (4 tiles per player; 16 tiles total). If 3 players, each player removes 2 stacks from one side of the woodpile (8 tiles per player; 24 tiles total). If 2 players, each player removes 3 stacks from one side of the woodpile (12 tiles per player; 24 tiles total).

Take the tiles you have removed from the woodpile and place them faceup.

The players examine their tiles. The first player tries to match one of his tiles with one turned up on the table having the same number of pips. If he is able to find a match, he places the pair faceup in front of him. Whether successful or not, he draws the top tile of the stack at the end of the woodpile from which the last stacks were drawn. Next, he attempts to match that tile with one on the table. If he is able to find a match, he removes the pair. If not, he places the tile drawn with those on the table.

The second player continues in the same way by attempting to match one of his tiles, then drawing a tile from the pile, and so on. The game continues until the pile is exhausted. A pair of 6-6 tiles in a player's hand is laid out at once.

The 2 tiles composing the supreme (2-1 and 4-2) pair with each other and form an exception to the rule in this game that all tiles having the same number of spots pair with each other without reference to their belonging to the civil or military series.

If a player holds a tile in his hand identical with 2 tiles on the table and the fourth tile of the same kind has not been played, he may, at his turn, pile the 3 tiles that are alike one on top of the other, faceup, at the opposite end of the stack from which tiles are being drawn. The player who plays the fourth tile then takes the other three.

When the last tile is drawn, players examine those they have taken. The tiles with 8 or more pips are called large fish and are worth 2 points for each pip of either color. The tiles with fewer than 8 pips are called "minnows"

and are worth 1 point for each red pip only. If the score of the minnows is between "tens," round the score up to the higher round number. For example, if the red pips on a player's minnows total 13 points, he earns a score of 20.

The player with the highest count becomes the winner and is paid by each of the players for each point he has in excess of their total.

Pai Gow

(Pai Gow is Cantonese; Pai Jo is Mandarin; aka Pai Kow)

This gambling game is an ancient Chinese or Korean domino game that has become very popular in quite a few Nevada, U.S., casinos. *Additional equipment needed:* 3 dice (to be thrown at the beginning of the game to determine the deal) and a number of chips of varying shapes denoting different denominations (or anything else that can be used for staking). Use chips during the game for staking and then settle accounts at the end of the game.

Object of the game: To have your high hand beat the banker's high hand and to have your low hand beat the banker's low hand.

Number of players: 4 players (one "banker" and three "punters") and any number of bystanders may participate.

Dominoes are stacked facedown in 2 piles, each pile containing 4 rows of 4 dominoes.

Each player takes a turn throwing 3 dice, going counterclockwise around the table and ending with the player who becomes the first banker, to determine where the deal begins. The dominoes are dealt by the banker, counterclockwise around the table, each player receiving 4 tiles.

Players examine their tiles without exposing them. From these tiles they form two separate hands of 2 tiles per hand: a high hand and a low hand, each designed to beat the banker's high hand and low hand. When the 3 players have placed their tiles on the table, they put their stake alongside. The banker may impose a limit if he wishes. Any onlooker may participate in the game by placing a stake alongside the tiles of a chosen player.

When all the stakes have been placed, the 3 players expose their first pair, their high hand. Next, the banker exposes his high hand. Then, the players expose their second pair, low hands. The banker follows by exposing his low hand.

To win a round, one of the three players or the banker must win both hands by holding a pair of tiles of higher standing than his opponents. If two different players win one hand each, the round is drawn and stakes are lifted from the table and may be staked again after the next deal. If the banker wins both hands, he takes all the stakes on the table. If a player wins both hands, the banker pays him his stake, and also those of any onlooker who may have laid a stake with him. The banker also

pays the other players and participating onlookers, if their pairs rate higher than both of his. If any player's pairs are lower than the banker's, the banker wins their stakes. There is no exchange between banker and a player unless the value of each pair is higher (or lower) on both hands.

When the gains and losses have been settled, the banker deals the second pile of 16 tiles. The second round is played in the same way.

When both rounds are finished, all the tiles are reshuffled and stacked in two piles of 16 dominoes each. The player on the banker's right becomes the new banker, and the game continues. Players may drop out at the end of any round and their place may be taken by an onlooker.

Tien Gow

(aka Tien Kow)

Additional equipment: 1 pair of dice to be thrown at the beginning of the game to determine the banker. *Number of players:* 4 players.

A banker is chosen by throwing dice. Eight tiles are dealt to each player by the banker. The players examine their tiles, then the banker leads by placing a tile faceup on the table.

The three players, in turn, follow counterclockwise around the table, each trying to take the trick with a tile of higher value than the others'. If a civil tile is led, the other players must follow with the same suit. If a player is unable to follow suit, he must discard a military tile. Similarly, if a military tile is led, the trick can only be taken by a military tile.

When a player wins the trick, he stacks the tiles in front of him and then leads the next trick with a tile from his hand. The game continues until all 8 tricks have been won.

The player who wins the final trick becomes the new banker and dealer for the next hand. If the banker wins the last trick, he remains banker; but the scoring of the new hand will be different, as described below.

After the last trick of each hand, the points are adjusted, usually by the exchange of counters. Then, the tiles are shuffled, stacked, and dealt by the new banker.

Instead of leading 1 tile, a player may lead 1 of the 16 named pairs or 1 of the 8 pairs comprised of:

6-6 and a mixed 9 (6-3 or 5-4)
1-1 and a mixed 8 (6-2 or 5-3)
4-4 and a mixed 7 (5-2 or 4-3)
3-1 and a mixed 5 (4-1 or 3-2)

The round can only be won by a pair of higher value. The Supreme Couple (2-1 and 4-2) only scores highest when it is led. Otherwise, it is the lowest of the pairs.

If a player wishes, he may lead with two pairs if it is his turn to lead. These can only be captured by two pairs of the same suit, civil or military, and one of the pairs must be of a higher value than either of those led.

Scoring: This is on a basic 4-point system:

• A player with no tricks loses 4

points to the winner of the last trick, who also becomes the new banker.

• A player with fewer than 4 tricks deducts this number from 4 and pays the difference to the winner of the last trick.

• A player winning 4 tricks does not win or lose any points.

• A player winning more than 4 tricks deducts 4 from the number and claims the difference from the winner of the last trick.

If a banker becomes the new banker, the basic figure in the second hand becomes 8 instead of 4; at a third deal, 12; at a fourth, 16; and so on. There is no limit to the number of times a banker may deal. There is usually an indicator on the table to show how many times the banker has dealt. When there is a new banker, the basic figure reverts to 4.

Extra points: If the banker leads the Supreme Couple, he claims a bonus of 4 points from each player. If a player leads the Supreme Couple, he claims a bonus of 4 points from the banker and 2 points from each of the other players.

If the banker leads any two of the following couples—6-6 and a mixed nine; 1-1 and a mixed eight; 4-4 and a mixed seven; 3-1 and a mixed five—he claims a bonus score of 8 points from each player. If a player makes the same lead, he wins 8 points from the banker and 4 points from each other player.

A game may finish at a set time or by mutual consent.

TWISTER: *Dragon Dance*

(© 1984 by Domino32 Company)

Number of players: 2 to 4 players.
Seven different results have been developed for this new game:

- Tornado: vertical head, vertical tail; head upward.
- Thunderbolt: vertical head, vertical tail; head downward.
- Joy: horizontal head, horizontal tail.
- Wildfire: horizontal head, vertical tail; tail upward.
- Floweret: horizontal head, vertical tail; tail downward.
- Hero: vertical head, horizontal tail; head upward.
- Misfortune: vertical head, horizontal tail; head downward.

Players take turns to place out their dominoes. The strategy is to match domino ends; try to block other players from matching domino ends.

The first domino placed (center, horizontal) is considered to be at the "sun" location.

Whenever a horizontal line reaches a length of 7 dominoes, change direction to vertical on either end. (One end always goes upward, the other downward.) Decide which vertical direction is "upward;" which is "downward."

Whenever a vertical line reaches a length of 3 dominoes, change direction to horizontal again.

The ever-bending domino line is, of course, always a continuous line.

It is quite difficult to complete a domino32 dragon. All dominoes must be used. Concentrate on the competition; try to win the game. Only when it is an absolute tie, can you have a complete dragon.

You will notice something very interesting: Your dragon surely does have a "head" and "tail" and is alive! At one end, there's a big head, at the other, a split tail. (The head is number (?)! The tail is number is (?)! Try it and find out the two numbers for yourself.)

Believe it or not! You may ma-

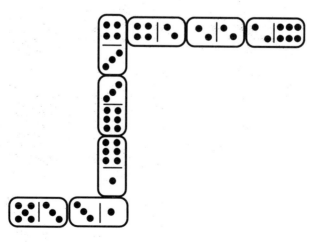

nipulate domino32 to see if you can ever make a whole dragon without a head or tail at its two ends. Isn't it a strange thing? Traditional domino play of 28 pieces can never do that! Why? Sorry, you'll have to ask a mathematician.

Now you can study what kind of dragon you players, as a group, have made. Check the head and tail numbers so as not to be confused. Remember, there are seven possible dragon-dance forms:

Vertical head, vertical tail; head upward: This is an evil dragon, a "tornado." Its tail hits the ground, causing great damage.

Vertical head, vertical tail; head downward: Another evil dragon, a "thunderbolt." You have made an aggressive dragon.

Horizontal head, horizontal tail: A peaceful dragon, easy-going and happy. We call it "joy."

Horizontal head, vertical tail; tail upward: This is a naughty dragon. You build a "wildfire."

Horizontal head, vertical tail; tail downward: What a dandy dragon. Is it a "floweret"?

Vertical head, horizontal tail; head upward: An alert and daring one. The name of this dragon is "hero."

Vertical head, horizontal tail; head downward: Unfortunately the dragon is sick. It is a "misfortune."

So you know what kind of team players you are, by observing the twister dance of the whole dragon you have made together, you will find whether your team is a tornado, a thunderbolt, a joy, a wildfire, a floweret, a hero, or a misfortune!

Another Word About Dominoes

Dominoes, as homespun and colloquial as they are, have now gone high-tech and are being bantered around on the Internet. Just as there are many ways and rules to play dominoes, there are that many ways of doing the same on the Internet with methods and players increasing daily.

Today, domino players can play domino games, buy domino sets, and discuss games in chat rooms, all over the Internet. Puremco, a major domino company, has a home page at Dominoes.com that can be used to purchase dominoes. And, as always on the Internet, each person with something to say about dominoes will gladly give you references and homesite addresses for many other domino game sites.

Some years ago, Curtis Cameron, a computer programmer from Texas, and a friend were discussing how a computer could be "taught" to play Forty-Two. After working on it about a year, he successfully created a game that ran in Microsoft Windows. In the game, a player is presented with a view of his own hand, and the computer decides which dominoes to play for the other 3 players. Cameron later came up with a second domino game. Today, he offers the two games as a package over his web page, and has been praised by quite a few experts as having the best domino games on the Internet.

Recently, Cameron added to his site the ability for two or more people on the Internet to connect together and play a game. Each person sees the same thing as when playing a computer opponent, but the plays are coming from the other person on the Internet. The critical step here is to find another person who is ready to play when you are. A utility called ICQ lets you build a list of people, and it will show you when someone is online and ready to play. At Cameron's web page, there is also a list of people who want to play. Isn't technology wonderful!

I hope that you have enjoyed this book as much as I have enjoyed writing it. If, through it, you have become an enthusiast and would like background on my researches into the games, information on current and new domino products, scheduled game tournaments or cruises, or other matters relating to the game of dominoes, you can reach me, Jennifer Kelley, at P.O. Box 21569, Waco, Texas 76710 (e-mail: DoublBlank@aol.com). (For requested responses by mail, please be kind enough to enclose a self-addressed stamped envelope.)

Game References

Party Games Good for Five or More Players

Chickenfoot	Use a double-9 or larger set.
Cyprus	Use a double-6 or larger set.
Domino Pool	Use a double-6 set.
The Fortress	Use a double-9 or larger set.
Mexican Train	Use a double-9 or larger set.
One-Arm Joe	Use a double-6 set.
Tiddle-a-Wink	Use double-6 or larger set.

Games Requiring Additional Dominoes or Tiles

Seventy-Nine	Use two sets of double-6.
Eighty	Use two sets of double-6.
Eighty-Four	Use two sets of double-6.
Eighty-Eight	Use two sets of double-6.
Fishing (Tiu u)	Use two sets of Oriental tiles.

Games Requiring Additional Items

Bullfighting	1 pair of dice—at start of game to determine banker
Collecting Tens	4 dice and a cup
Domino Pool	coins, dried beans, poker chips for use in wagering
Mexican Train	coins, dried beans, poker chips for use as markers
Pai Gow	3 dice, and chips or other such items of varying shapes or colors, to denote different denominations and used for stakes
Tien Gow	1 pair of dice—at start of game to determine banker

Bidding Variations of Game of Forty-Two

Big Bertha
Cajun Hokey Pokey
Eagle Eye
East Lansing Deferred-Style Nillo
Follow Me
Inverted Low Boy
Low
Low Boy
Multiple Trumps Forty-Two
Naperville Onesies
Near-Seven
Nel-o or Nillo (given)
No Catchem
No Trump
Plunge (given)
Sevens (given)
Splash
West Texas Rules

Cross-Reference of Oriental Games

K'ap T'ai Shap (Collecting Tens)
Pai Gow (Pai Jo, Pai Kow)
Tau Ngau (Bullfighting)
Tien Gow (Tien Kow)
Tiu u (Fishing)
Ts'ung Shap (Disputing Tens)

Index

About the Author

Jennifer Kelley is an enthusiastic writer who has fallen in love with dominoes. Recently, *Highways* magazine published her article on domino-playing campers (game playing is a favorite pastime, growing particularly among the RV crowd). She also took the time, in the midst of preparing this book for publication, to host a successful First Annual (1999) Domino Games and Open House in Katy, Texas, with tournaments on Five-Up, Cuban Dominoes, and Forty-Two.

Jennifer publishes an international newsletter, DomiNews, for those, she says, "who wish to enjoy a competitive edge over other domino enthusiasts and those who just love domino games," and delights in learning about and passing along fascinating tidbits on the expanding domino world.

Jennifer Kelley and her family live in Katy, Texas.